SUCCESS OR FAILURE
YOU DECIDE

SUCCESS OR FAILURE

YOU DECIDE

Audel Acevedo

LATINO Book Publisher
EDITORIAL Autores Latinos

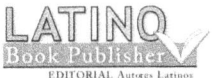

Mesa, Arizona | 2016

First Edition

Cover and book design by Yolie Hernandez | HISI
Cover and author pictures by Francesca Elena Garza
Free Light Photos | photographeraz.com

Published by Latino Book Publisher, an imprint of HISI.
No part of this book may be used, saved, scanned, or reproduced in any manner whatsoever without the written permission of the author and/or publisher.
All Rights Reserved.

Latino Book Publisher | HISI
PO Box 50553
Mesa, Arizona 85208-0028
(480) 646-9401 | hisi.org | info@hisi.org

Success or Failure: You Decide
Copyright © 2016 Audel Acevedo
1st. ed. pp.226

Paperback ISBN 13: 978-1-936885-17-6
Printed in the United States of America.

DISCLAIMER: Opinions expressed in this book are those of the author, and do not reflect the publisher's opinions. Information written by the author reflects his personal experiences and views, and is only intended as reading material. This book is not intended as a substitute for professional counseling from health care professionals. Readers should consult a professional counselor concerning their mental health, and particularly with respect to any symptoms that may require professional attention.

Dedication

I dedicate this book to the leader of the band, my father Audel Acevedo Sr. Although he is no longer physically with me, his wise advice still guides me, and I still strive to make him proud, as if he was still here. I believe he is still here in spirit watching over me; I can feel his energy.

I also dedicate the book to my beautiful wife, Laura Acevedo, who has stuck with me through thick and thin, through good times and not so good times; I could not have done it without her support. She believed in me when no one else did, so I would like to quote my favorite song from Kenny Rogers: *"And she believes in me, I'll never know just what she sees in me..."*

This book is also dedicated to all my children who have inspired me the most: Corina, Lolita, Alexis, Audel, Daisy, and last but not least, Leslie (Minime). I thank God each and every day for these six beautiful blessings. I feel very fortunate and proud of each and every one of them. I love them all and I am grateful for the lessons they have taught me.

Acknowledgements

I would like to thank and acknowledge my publisher Latino Book Publisher—Yolie Hernandez and her team—for their support and guidance, and all the hard work they put into this book. I don't know what I would have done without them. Thanks to them my book is now a reality. After all these years of writing, proofreading and editing, my book has materialized, and another dream has come true.

I would also like to thank a group of unsung heroes, our frontline classroom soldiers who dedicate their life to teach, to coach and to mentor: our teachers. Thank you and God bless you. Keep on teaching, for when we teach we learn and when we learn we grow.

CONTENTS

WHAT YOU WILL FIND INSIDE

Introduction ... 13

Success ... 17

Destiny ... 28

Vision ... 31

Imagination ... 33

Faith And Belief ... 36

Focus ... 38

Accountability ... 39

Love ... 41

Harmony ... 42

Passion ... 43

Ambition ... 44

Enthusiasm ... 46

Self-Improvement ... 48

Determination ... 51

Achievement ... 54

Potential ... 57

Manners ... 59

Responsibility ... 67

Attitude ... 69

Purpose ... 72

Discipline ... 73

Motivation ... 75

Resiliency ... 77

Avoiding Mistakes ... 78

Harmony ... 80

Happiness ... 81

Music ... 83

CORE VALUES ... 84	CAUTION ... 129
INTEGRITY ... 86	LAWS ... 131
WORK ETHIC ... 88	PROBLEMS ... 132
HEALTH ... 91	TEMPTATION ... 134
HUMILITY ... 92	WRONG CROWDS ... 135
ACCEPTANCE ... 93	CONFLICTS ... 137
BENEVOLENCE ... 95	PEER PRESSURE ... 139
GRATEFULNESS ... 98	BULLYING ... 141
FRIENDSHIPS ... 100	RISKS ... 143
PUNCTUALITY ... 102	HATE ... 147
TIME ... 103	CONFRONTATIONS ... 148
TIME FRAMES ... 104	ANGER ... 149
URGENCY ... 105	AGGRESSION AND RETALIATION ... 151
TAKE CHARGE ... 106	BAD ... 153
PLAN ... 112	TRUTHFULNESS ... 155
PREPARE ... 115	COMMUNICATION ... 156
STRATEGY ... 116	TEACHERS ... 158
ACTION ... 118	BOOKS ... 160
QUALITY ... 120	EDUCATION ... 161
DEDICATION ... 121	PROACTIVE ... 165
ENERGY ... 123	LEADERSHIP ... 167
EFFORT ... 125	CHANGE ... 169
ADVANTAGE ... 126	LEAVING ... 171
RESOURCES ... 127	

Appearances ... 172

Assumptions ... 173

Image ... 174

Critical Thinking ... 175

Fear ... 176

Challenges ... 178

Opportunities ... 180

Character ... 181

Personality ... 182

Moving On ... 183

Confidence ... 185

Taking Responsibility ... 186

Maturity ... 188

Doing The
Right Thing ... 190

Criticism ... 191

Perception ... 193

Reliability ... 194

Contentment ... 195

Good Habits ... 197

Composure ... 199

Inspiration ... 200

Parents ... 201

Faults ... 204

Risky Trends ... 206

Reflections ... 210

Open Your Eyes ... 213

SUCCESS OR FAILURE: YOU DECIDE

*I*t is my hope that this book *Success or Failure: You Decide* will assist young people in making the right decisions, and guide them when they feel alone, confused or unsure on how to act, who to turn to, what to do or how to behave.

Some of the contents in this book perhaps will sound familiar to you, or you may have heard them before but never paid much attention to them. Maybe you felt they did not matter, they did not interest you, or thought they did not apply to you. Perhaps you felt they were not important, but they are. As you read this book some things might be new to you, but whether they are new to you or not, the goal is to give you encouragement to make changes in your attitude toward life, and help you become a better person. This will result in more opportunities in your life, and help you become more successful at whatever your definition of success may be, or at whatever your passion may be.

Following the instructions in this book will increase your chances of being successful and having a happy life. As you practice what you learn, you will begin to see positive results in your life. It will help you to be clear about what you want, and to not lower your standards just to please others. Leave all negative people, bad habits, negative thoughts behind, and everything else that can bind you.

We never get anywhere by accident. Something takes us there, whether it may be our own actions, or by allowing others' actions affect our lives. Life is about evolving, graduating, advancing, and taking it to the next level, but not in a negative way. Some call it evolving, but too often young people take the wrong route at an early age. Hopefully this book will help you overcome some of life's obstacles and avoid common pitfalls, as well as keep you from making ordinary mistakes, either out of ignorance or arrogance. Always remember: You do have options, so make good choices. Sometimes when a young person gets in trouble their first response is: "I had no choice," or "I had to do it." This is a big myth. You always have a choice. You can walk away, you can say no, but you do have a choice. You will always have choices; life is full of choices.

Success or Failure: You Decide is not meant to help you achieve great power or wealth. It is more about leading a productive and happy life, succeeding and achieving your goals whatever they may be. This book intends to help you stay safe. It is full of useful information and instructions that will help you in life. Think of it as a "how to manual," on how to put something together, or how to make it function properly. Often we try to go through life without following instructions because we believe we know everything, how things work or are supposed to work. Only to find out we were wrong all along. How many times have we bought something new and tried to put it together without reading the instructions, just to end up breaking it because we failed to follow the instructions? It is only after we have failed that we begin looking at the manual to see what we did wrong. Wouldn't it be great if we had a manual that could prepare us for life before we make those mistakes and guide us through life? A guidebook that could tell us what to do before we make those common mistakes?

This book is organized in easy-to-read-and-understand sections that you can reference quickly. You will find basic answers to most common questions; it can be your companion in time of need, when you are lonely and have no one to turn to for advice, someone you can turn to when confused or have a question. When you feel lost, or when all of a sudden a situation presents itself and you do not know how to react, or know how to handle it. Following life's instructions will make you a better person, better citizen, student, a better all-around human being. It's meant to help you live a safe, happy and successful life. *Success or Failure: You Decide*, will assist you along the way and help you make the right decisions. This is my only goal. But keep in mind that you have to practice what you read and learn. Put it to the test and to work, and remember that reading all the books in the world will not be of any help unless you put what you read into practice and are willing to make a change in your life.

LIVE TO SUCCEED. NOT JUST TO SURVIVE

To succeed you have to have a strong desire for success, and to continue succeeding you have to maintain that desire. Most people need to begin from the very bottom and work up, given that success is an uphill battle; most likely you'll need to work your way up. To succeed you need to climb the ladder, the stairs; there is no elevator. Succeeding will demand effort, courage, a meaningful purpose, and strong direction. Don't measure success by how far you have come, but by what you had to overcome to arrive.

Young people, success begins with an education that prepares you for professional success. Staying in school and never saying "I don't need an education" are two key elements you must do. Without an education you will be unprepared for a highly competitive world where people with college degrees apply for and get the best jobs. An American World number one professional tennis player said, "Success is not a destination; it is a journey." Success is also a choice; you choose success or failure. So you see, success does not happen by accident. To succeed you need knowledge, a strategy and to take action.

Let's be real: With success you will face struggles and challenges; without struggle there is no challenge, and without a challenge there is no success. Difficulties produce challenges; if there were no challenges everyone would be doing it. Success without challenges would be worthless, and life would be very boring. The road to success is not always easy, it requires sacrifice, hard work, dedication, commitment and perseverance; there are no shortcuts. An actor and film producer believes: "You can only live your dream by working hard towards it. That's living your dream." If you want it bad enough you will achieve success, but nothing is going to fall into your lap, you'll have to work for it. How bad do you want it? While you may be sitting around saying it cannot be done, others are already doing it. Or while you are sitting around saying you will never make it, others are already making it. Some young people often excuse themselves by saying that very successful people like Steve Jobs (Apple), Mark Zuckerberg (Facebook), Bill Gates (Microsoft), Walt Disney (Disneyland) and Abraham Lincoln (U.S. President) turned out just fine and achieved a great deal without formal education. However, these individuals are the exception and they too faced many challenges, had to build new and different ways to learn and develop the skills to become successful, and they demonstrated a strong desire to learn and be independent thinkers. The path to success is generally through education, and teachers are your transportation, so get on board. Education is your ticket to success, and it is a matter of choice, just like education and intelligence are a matter of choice. You can choose intelligence over ignorance and success over failure by educating yourself.

When you start climbing the success ladder try not to trample over others, or leave anyone behind. Care for the people who cared for you. Share the success, the fruit of your labor, and never let success go to your head or become greedy. Spread your good fortune, do not stop to admire your work until you are at the top, and once you reach the top don't forget to help those approaching behind you. Control your progress, know when to slow down, speed up, stop or rest and wait for the right moment to act. The road to success will always be under construction. Measure your own success, don't allow others to measure or determine it for you. Never compare your success to others' because success is not always measured by wealth; it's more about personal growth, achievements and overcoming obstacles. You determine your own success, progress and achievements. Success requires sacrifice and cost: You pay with hard work, sweat, tears, dedication, and if at first you fail, try and try again. Eventually your hard work will pay off. Never become discouraged.

Work on sharpening your skills and perfecting your trade. Ask yourself: Do I just want to survive, or do I want to succeed? Success requires sacrifice, sometimes you need to sacrifice one thing to gain another. Like the saying goes, no pain no gain.

Do not be a materialistic person. Being materialistic means that you are excessively concerned with material possessions; or money-oriented. How much do you really want or need? Don't be enslaved to material things. Success is not all about money; it's about your love for the things you want, your passion. Make it fun and enjoyable; successful people know the importance of an education, health, and family. They know this is part of the recipe for success, to make it big you need to dream big.

Leave your mark in life; in order to achieve this, you must give your best. Each failure brings you closer to success. Success is losing and failing without losing your enthusiasm; life does not reward mediocrity, so bring your best to make the grade. Success also means you have conquered and achieved the desired result. You overcame and prospered in the face of adversity. You made it!

The choices you make, not circumstances, determine your success. Success is never a straight line it has twists and turns, ups and downs. It's about doing what you love and being good at it, and being able to say "In my life I did what I loved and I enjoyed every minute of it!" Undertaking anything other than what you love will only bring you stress and depression regardless of how much money you make.

Life is a puzzle and all the pieces are in front of you, just position them together. Everyone wants to go to heaven but nobody wants to die. Same with success: Everybody wants to succeed but not many want to pay the price and work for it. Be persistent, never give up no matter what; remember to savor victory you have to experience defeat. Nothing comes to those who wait, this is a myth; success comes to those who make things happen. You need to have the desire to succeed. In order to succeed you need to not fear failure, since some of the best lessons are learned from failure. One more failure means you are one more step closer to reaching your goal. Just like a salesman who will only make one out of ten sales attempts, but it is those nine non-sales, the nine stepping stones that will get him that one successful sale.

Success means you are proud of your accomplishments and satisfied with the results, and that you are living life according to your terms because in the end, material things, money, and other earthly treasures will not matter much. What does matter is your family, your health, your real friends, and all the precious moments you share. Success means you are enjoying life, living your life to the fullest, and having no regrets. Laughing, crying, singing, joking, sharing your good fortune, planting a tree and smelling the roses while thanking God along the way for all the good and bad times that will teach you the most valuable lessons, so in the end you can say, "Wow, what a ride!"

Success is not just about reaching a destination; it is also about how many people you help along the way. It is measured in happiness, and not in material possessions. You define your own success; don't let others define it for you. Success is an award given to those who work hard, who dream, dare, and have the courage to never give up. It is celebrating each and every day and not waiting until the end. Success is like a mountain that does not come to you or move; you have to go to the mountain to conquer it. You will be required to leave all comforts behind and make sacrifices. Some people only have hopes and wishes, but successful people have dreams, goals, desires, and plans to succeed.

Bring out the entrepreneur in you and find your niche. Use the tools that God gave you and make do with what you possess. Innovate, improvise, do what you love, and love what you do. To succeed never give less than one hundred percent; winners never quit and quitters never win. Even when quitting seems as an easy alternative and your goals may seem so far away, don't quit! Each strike will bring you closer to that home run; each missed kick will bring you closer to your goal. If you want to succeed you need to work and desire it, and that drive can only derive from within you. The number one ingredient for success is hard work: hoping, dreaming, desiring, envisioning, are nothing without hard work. You must always have a burning desire to succeed and not let it burn out; fan the flame. Success starts when you have the courage to leave your comfort zone. You need to have love for your work, the ability to endure through sweat, tears, pain, hunger, and sacrifice for success to follow. Sacrifice today to achieve success tomorrow. In order to succeed everyone needs to pull in the same direction, work for the same cause, and always have a positive attitude. You create your own future and destiny. Fortune lies in your hands. Some people just want to survive, but others want to succeed. Which one are you?

Success means you are in position to help others, and this is a privilege. There is no easy way to succeed except through hard work; all successful people had to pay their dues in order to attain success. But never sacrifice your health, your family, or your dignity for the sake of success. To succeed you need to have the desire, the commitment, the devotion and passion for what you do, and you must have a plan. Success is not about being rich and famous; it's more about just being happy. Success is living life according to your values, and your life needs to reflect those values.

Only ask and receive advice from people who have arrived where you want to be, as well as positive people and not negative or pessimistic individuals. The secret is not only asking the right questions, but asking the right people. Do not be afraid to ask and do not be afraid of the answers, no matter how cruel the answers may be. Honest people will tell you what you need to hear, which is the truth and not what you want to hear. Do not feel intimidated by people who you may feel are above you or are more intelligent or wealthier than you. Do not be intimidated by their grandeur since none of this matters; learn from their lessons and allow this to motivate you to achieve more, to surpass them; yes, you can do it! Do not be afraid to wander into uncharted territory, be an innovator; do not be afraid to try new things, be an entrepreneur.

Do not let others discourage you from achieving your dreams, goals, and your success. Pay no attention to barking dogs. If you go through life throwing stones at every dog that barks, you will never reach your destination. Stick to your mission, purpose, and plan no matter what. Do not stop to argue with ignorant people along the way. Remember, you have a purpose; you are going places, so do not let anything stop you.

If you are serious about your success and about making something out of your life, then take life seriously, every aspect of your life: health, education and career, as well as family, faith and God. With faith all things are possible. Life is not what it is; life is what you make of it. All things are within your reach: success, wealth, education, love and happiness. The possibilities are endless, and there are no limitations, only the ones you set on yourself. Success, faith and God have no limits, and you have no limits. Pursue your dreams, let your imagination flow.

You can have whatever your heart desires. But you have to really want it, and have the faith to attain it. Make a commitment to yourself that you will not stop until you achieve your goal, that you will not give up come what may. Success is within everyone's reach. It doesn't matter who you are, what you are, where you are, what you have, where you are from, or the color of your skin; none of it matters. Success does not discriminate; it is within everyone's reach.

Successful people have a great attitude, versus those who fail due to their negative attitude. Successful individuals are positive in their thinking, they are happy, full of joy and love, and they believe in themselves which results in success. They had all these qualities before they became successful, not the other way around. Success originates inside you, it comes from within, and your attitude determines whether you succeed or fail. A positive attitude is important to succeed. If you look around you will see that all successful people have a few things in common: They are very positive, they believe in themselves, they do not give up on the first try, or the second or the third try, they continue until they finally break through and finally make it. They overcome obstacles, they fall down numerous times, but they get up time, and time again, they keep getting back up more determined than before, just as optimistic and passionate as before, and all because they are hungry for success. They have a goal. They have a mission and a dream, and they are determined to reach it no matter what. They make every effort, place all their time and energy into it, and every drop of sweat that they have. They come to win not to just play because success, just like winning, takes one hundred ten percent; anything less is just competing. To succeed you must be willing to dedicate that extra ten percent; this is why only one percent succeeds, the remaining ninety-nine percent are not willing to give that extra ten percent.

Anyone and everyone can find success in life. The past does not matter, what does matter is what you do from this point on. Focus on your future and start working towards your goals now. It is your future, so do not waste time on things that are not important, that will not contribute towards obtaining your goals and your end result. If your goal is happiness and you are happy, then you have already succeeded. Success represents different things to different people; you need to define your own success. If your goals have been accomplished, you have succeeded. If your outcome is favorable you have succeeded. If the results of your mission are positive, you have succeeded. If you are happy with what you are doing now, then you have already reached success.

We sometimes ask ourselves why some succeed while others do not. Well, let's review, let's take a closer examination. The answer may be that those who you see and are successful are those individuals who do not lose sight of their dreams, goals and objectives. They do not waste valuable time on things that do not matter, and things that are not going to help their cause. All their effort, energy, and focus are concentrated on reaching their dreams and achieving their goals. They focus on the subject at hand and do not get sidetracked with other nonsense. Take the following example for instance: If your passion is football, if this is your real dream, your goal, then you should block everything else out of your life, everything, except football. You eat, sleep, and breathe football. You sleep with the pigskin by your side, get to know it, what it weighs and the max air pressure, what the dimensions are, and how far it travels. You carry the football with you wherever you go, you practice at every opportunity, you watch all games including high school games, college and NFL games. You record the games, watch them over and over again, and take notes. You get to know the players, their history, methods, advice, you learn the plays, the rules, read anything related to football, and do not waste valuable time on other stuff not related to football. One hundred percent of your mind is occupied by football and nothing else matters. You hang out with people with like interests, attend trainings, camps, practice in your spare time, and are always working on improving your game. You may now be asking if this is not too much football, and the answer is no, not if you are serious. Not if you want to succeed in football or whatever your goal is, you have to dedicate yourself entirely. That is if you are really serious about your success, then you have to make sacrifices. No more activities or leisure time for you, besides your education your entire life revolves around your goal, football. Your training regimen takes center stage above all other activities because success takes sweat, scrapes, bruises, strict diets, hard work, dedication and discipline. Because if you want it bad enough you will achieve it; remember, success costs and this is where you start paying. You may be asked to give a little extra, that ten percent will get you to the top. You need to have the desire to succeed, reach deep inside within you, and give it all you have; this is the difference between successful and unsuccessful people. Those who do not succeed only go halfway, they never seem to finish things and make excuses, they are not dedicated entirely to their cause and become discouraged and quit very easily when faced with adversity. So in order to be successful you need to dedicate yourself to one goal. Work on perfecting your trade, do not jump around from one thing to another, from one job to another, stick with it through thick and thin, and start from the bottom and work your way up. For example, if you start to work at a restaurant you may need to start as a dishwasher, then work your way up to waiter, cook, chef, manager, and eventually owner. If you are in construction, learn the trade and start as a laborer, then on to crew leader, foreman, supervisor, manager, president, partner, and eventually owner. You need to stick with it just like in football, with hard work and dedication you will get there, just do not become discouraged.

Often we see the younger generation jump from job to job, not lasting more than a month or so, and it would seem like every time you see or talk to some people they are doing something different from the last time you saw them. When you ask them why they left, their answers vary: "It was not working out," "it wasn't fun," "it was boring," "too much work," "not enough money, "too many hours, "no days off," and so on. Often they just quit without giving notice, or not having anything else to fall back on. They will never know if it would have worked out since they did not stay with it long enough and pay their dues. So you need to start somewhere and build a decent employment resume, with a suitable work history. Make that resume look good, learn the trade and eventually those higher paying jobs will come along but you need to have ambition, the desire to succeed, like wanting your bosses job and his salary. But you have to be prepared for when that opportunity arises, always be looking to move up in your career and in your life.

DESTINY

DREAM. VISUALIZE. BELIEVE. AND CREATE

*L*ife begins with a dream, a vision, and a belief that results in a creation. Life is about creating our own destiny. As human beings, every decision we make in our lives brings us to our present circumstances. For you, as a young person, your current situation is not your final destination, and it is an ever-changing process.

Destiny is where you bring yourself, not where life brings you, and have yet to go. Destiny is creative work, and as individuals we are the only ones who can create it. You, and only you, are responsible for how you shape your own destiny and for the changes you have to make. Young woman, young man, you are the only one who builds your own life and world, and building both is based on your terms and the desires of your heart. You can create your own future. But that is also based on your thoughts and feelings: What you think about now and what you feel today is what you will become tomorrow.

Your thoughts, dreams, feelings, and visions will eventually become your world and new reality. Just ask and you will receive. If you believe you will receive: if you truly believe it, you will receive. As with everything in life, especially as a young person, you must practice positive thinking. Always think in a positive way. Having positive and high expectations in everything you do is necessary. Always make the power of positive thinking work for you. Each of us writes our very own unique story of our life, from the very first chapter to the final one. You are the author of your own personal book, the book of your life; the pages of your book are blank, so today write how you want your life to be tomorrow. As human beings we have choices; whatever we choose to think and to believe is what our lives will become. Every thought and feeling is creating your future that will eventually materialize and draw everything into your life: good, bad, or indifferent. Visualize this as a magnet: Its magnetism attracts metal objects. Therefore, in order to succeed, all your actions need to reflect your positive thoughts, emotions, and desires. Today you are the person you imagined yesterday. You are a by-product of your very own thoughts and actions; you are the architect of your life and the designer of your destiny. You need to live your life with a plan, dreams, faith, hope, and purpose. Always remember: You are what you dream, visualize, believe, and create.

Expectations in life are an important ingredient of our destiny. We are what we expect of ourselves. Some people think that by changing the school they attend or their job, their luck will change overnight. They go great distances looking for success when success could be right in front of them, and they do not even see it. Moving from place to place without a plan, direction, or purpose —just randomly moving somewhere else— will not bring instant success or luck; you must have a plan and be willing to develop it. What is success? Success is what you want it to be, but it takes dedication and hard work to achieve it. Add love and passion to the mix, and success is sure to follow.

To succeed there is no such thing as "luck" or "fortune." We create our own luck and fortune by our actions. Trying to succeed without hard work is like trying to harvest something that was not first sowed. Yes, having talents is important, but they don't mean much without hard work and dedication; this is the reason why some very talented people fail while others succeed. Success also involves being persistence, not giving up at the first encounter of adversity. In fact, regardless of what you encounter in life, you must keep on going. This is called persistence. If you think your success is possible and you believe, it will happen. Success is attainable when you also possess the desire and courage to achieve it.

So what are the key ingredients for success? Hard work, vision, dedication, determination, and persistence. What you expect is what you receive. Be in control of your own environment, keep expectations and beliefs at a high level, preserve the faith, and continue dreaming and visualizing. Create your destiny.

WHAT WE ENVISION TODAY WE WILL BE DOING TOMORROW

A person without a vision perishes. The meaning of this principle is that having a vision and purpose in our lives is essential. See what others cannot visualize and then share your vision. Foreseeing new opportunities takes effort. Focusing all your energy on your vision is necessary, and although you lack the ability to control your background, there is something you can do: Control the direction where you want to go. From this point on, taking charge of the steering wheel of the vehicle called destiny is also necessary. Steer in the direction where you want to go, not where the road wants to take you. Remember that destiny is a creative work, and you are responsible for creating it. We choose the kind of person we want to become. Therefore, what we envision makes us who we are and gives us our place in life.

We can do whatever we set our minds to. All human creations, accomplishments, and great inventions were born from a thought, a vision, or a dream. Look at your surroundings: Everything around you began in someone's mind as a dream, a vision, or a thought. The house where you live, the clothes you wear, and the car you drive: All began in the mind of a visionary, a thinker, or a dreamer. The vision you have of your future is what you will be doing. Wherever you envision your future self is where you will be.

Never underestimate the power of your mind, your magnetism and attraction, your imagination and vision. What you give you will receive. If you give love you will receive love. If you give joy that's what you will receive. Conversely, hate will bring you hate. Our lives are a reflection of us; a mirror effect.

As a young person, having a vision will lead you to achieve what you visualize. It often begins with just a simple vision. Form an image in your mind of what you aim toward in life, continuously think about it and it will become true. Having faith, being a positive person, and persistently working on your vision will lead you to accomplish it, one step at a time, one day at a time.

WHERE CREATIVITY BEGINS

*I*magine what could be. Imagine the possibilities. Picture it in your mind; this is where it all starts, in our imagination. We need to have imagination in order to visualize ideas and form images in our minds, whatever our concepts may be. Imagine how beautiful life could be. Think with imagination and inventiveness, this is how creativity begins. How can you improve something and make it better? If you can imagine and dream something, you can accomplish it. There is practically no limits, so dream big and aim high; the sky's the limit. All great things in life began in someone's imagination. Thoughts, visions or dreams is where it all begins. So in order to succeed in life, you need to make sure you put your imagination to work.

Accomplishing your goals won't just happen. As with everything in life, you need to aim toward an objective. Draw a straight line to what you want and do not stray. After you reach one goal, set up another one, and then another one. Aim high, shoot for the stars but also be realistic. Having realistic goals is necessary. Kidding yourself and living in a fantasy world doesn't accomplish real goals. Ask yourself what it is that you hope to accomplish in life and what you need to help you reach your destination. Then, set short-term and long-term goals, and establish steps to get you there. Use measuring sticks to check your progress. Prepare yourself, and seek people who will assist you in reaching your goals. Accountability is fundamental: Who will hold you accountable?

Focus all your energy on your goals, and be persistent. Work at it until you are capable, and then always strive to improve and become better. Do not give up no matter what. If you truly want something, you will achieve it, if you believe in you. If this is your mission, you will succeed, and once you reach your goals decide to either continue or move on to the next goal. Be ambitious, but do not become greedy, and never compromise your goals just to please others. Remember that having goals and targets will give you a sense of direction. Think of it as a map for your life: It will give you guidance, tell you where you are and where you are headed. This will also help you advance, prevent you from going around in circles and getting stuck. Answer the following questions to help you get a sense of direction that will help you attain your goals: Where have I been? Where am I now? And, where am I going?

Goals are like good friends: You can never have enough. Having a good amount of goals and ensuring you come up with more as you go will give meaning to your life and reasons to live for. Goals can be anything from just being generally happy, to learning a new foreign language or getting a college degree. If you really love something work hard to retain it, and don't let it go. Holding on to your goals and dreams will ensure you keep possession of them. Take into account that dreams do not come with expiration dates. So dream on, dream big and carry big goals. Then go out and diligently make your dreams come true. Dream as if you are living forever, keep sight of your dreams, and if at first you do not succeed, try and try again until you do.

Always focus on your goals because focusing is one of the things that really matters. Set your mind to it, and leave what you do not want out of the equation. Abandon all useless activities and anything that will not help you arrive to the end result. If it does not fit within your plan then leave it out. This even includes people who are not part of your plan, or who are not willing to support your cause or contribute to your goals.

In life we need to have dreams and plenty of them. Never stop dreaming but remember that for dreams to work, you need to make them work. To catch a dream you need to chase it. Good things do not come to those who are passive; good things come to those who work diligently. Dreams need action to become a reality. You need to share your dreams and vision, for all great accomplishments started as someone's dream, so dream big! Keep in mind that the beauty is in the journey not just in the destination.

As you image your life's possibilities and set realistic goals and work to accomplish them, remember to also pause and enjoy the journey, the scenery, and the people along the way.

FAITH AND BELIEF

BELIEVE IT. ACHIEVE IT. LIVE IT.

You can achieve anything you set your mind to. It all begins with a belief; if you believe you can, you are half way there, but you need to believe. Have you ever wondered why some people succeed at everything while others seem to fail at everything? Well, the answer may lie in how people perceive things, how much they believe in themselves and on what they set out to do. Everything begins in our minds, so you need to believe that you can.

Visualize what you want, have faith, be optimistic, stay positive, do it with love, and everything will fall into place. Believe, and everything will be okay. Believe in you and all you do. Believe in God, in family, in your abilities and capabilities, your training, your dreams, your goals, and your cause. Be hopeful and confident about the future, look for the positive sides, and focus on people's qualities not on their flaws. Always believe you are capable. If you believe you can, then you will be right; if you believe you cannot, then you will be right as well.

Believe in yourself because if you don't, then nobody else will. If you don't believe in yourself, you might as well pack up and go home.

Young man and woman, have faith in what you want to achieve. Have complete trust and confidence that it can be done, that it will happen. Have faith and be positive, be hopeful in what you do, and do everything with love. Be open to all possibilities. Believe it, achieve it, live it. With faith, prosperity, abundance and happiness are all possible. Believing will also help you fulfill your life's desires, but faith and hard work are necessary. Believe it can be done and fight for what you believe in. Fight for your goals and your dreams.

Keep in mind that to achieve anything in life requires consistency, which means that all your actions need to reflect your thoughts; you cannot be thinking one thing while doing something else. Once you set your mind to do something, go for it and do not look back! You can do whatever you set your mind to. You can accomplish anything in life; you only have to believe it.

BEING ATTENTIVE TO ONE POINT

Place all of your focus on your goals, avoid distractions at all costs, and pay attention to what you are doing. Focusing means you are directing your efforts and being attentive to one point. Remember to reach a goal, you need to draw a straight line to your target and not allow yourself to be sidetracked. Concentrate on the task at hand, on one subject at a time, and block everything else out.

To focus it is necessary to avoid people that just seem to drain time and energy from you, and things that cause you to lose focus of your goals. Eat, sleep, and breathe your goals; pay close attention to the end result.

ACCEPTING RESPONSIBILITY

As a young person, it is very important that you understand and accept that you need to be accountable for your actions. Being accountable means an obligation or willingness to accept responsibility or to account for your actions.

Accountability will be expected from you whether you are at home, school, work or in public. Generally, you will be accountable for your actions to parents, teachers, friends and government officials. If something is entrusted in your care, you will be held accountable for the results.

Accountability is not only for adults. Employees, for example, have to answer for budget deficits, losses, liabilities, and their conduct at work. In life, we are held accountable for all of our actions. We have to answer for what we do, and sometimes for what we do not do. This is no different for young people.

Young men and women are responsible for the positive and negative outcomes of the choices they make. At school, you are expected to respect your teachers and classmates, and for turning in your assignments on time. When you drive a vehicle, you are responsible to make a stop when you see a red light. If you don't, you can be held accountable for causing an accident, hurting someone or damaging property, or at least paying a fine for running the red light. In this example, you can be held accountable by having your drivers' license privilege suspended.

Nowadays it seems as if everybody is watching us. Perhaps you or your friends have recorded a video with your mobile phone when you saw somebody doing something bad or illegal. In the same way, someone may be watching you, and you can be held accountable.

Show accountability by taking responsibility for your own actions. Stepping up and admitting you failed to do your responsibility is a way to show accountability.

LOVE MOVES MOUNTAINS

*L*ove is all we need. With love all is possible; love moves mountains and cures many ills. We must do everything with love. By loving everything we do we will always attain perfect results.

Love your school, your work, your friends, your family, your relationships, your neighborhood, and your environment, but most importantly you need to love yourself, because you cannot give what you do not possess. So whatever you do, make sure it is done with love and passion, and don't take love for granted. Love the world and your fellow human being. Do not take anything for granted, promote, and nurture love. If you love what you do you will succeed.

Love needs to be nurtured. If the grass seems greener on the other side, it's probably because it is loved, well cared for, and it receives the love and attention it deserves. Yes it is greener, but not by accident.

Love God and love everything you do. Love conquers all. With love all is possible.

HARMONY

MAKE EVERYTHING FIT INTO PLACE

*A*lways do your very best to live in harmony with nature, your fellow human being, and the environment. Maintain that harmony throughout your life with everything that surrounds you, with peace and a positive attitude. Make everything fit into place like a perfect puzzle just like God intended it to be. Everything has its place in life.

FIND WHAT FILLS YOU WITH PASSION

*P*assion is another indispensable quality to achieve success in our lives. Do you have an intense desire or enthusiasm for something? Then you have passion! As a young person you must have a personal drive or force to do things and achieve your goals, a desire to improve. Whatever you do in life, do it with passion and everything will fall into place. Be passionate about what you do: your work, your education, and your relationships. If you get a job because you love it, and not just for the paycheck, it'll be a lot easier to get out of bed in the morning, you'll be happier in your work, and happier in general. Believe in what you do, and find your passion. If you find you are not passionate about what you are presently doing, then it's time to make some changes in your life. Finding what fills you with passion and makes you happy, as well as what motivates you, will position you on the path to success.

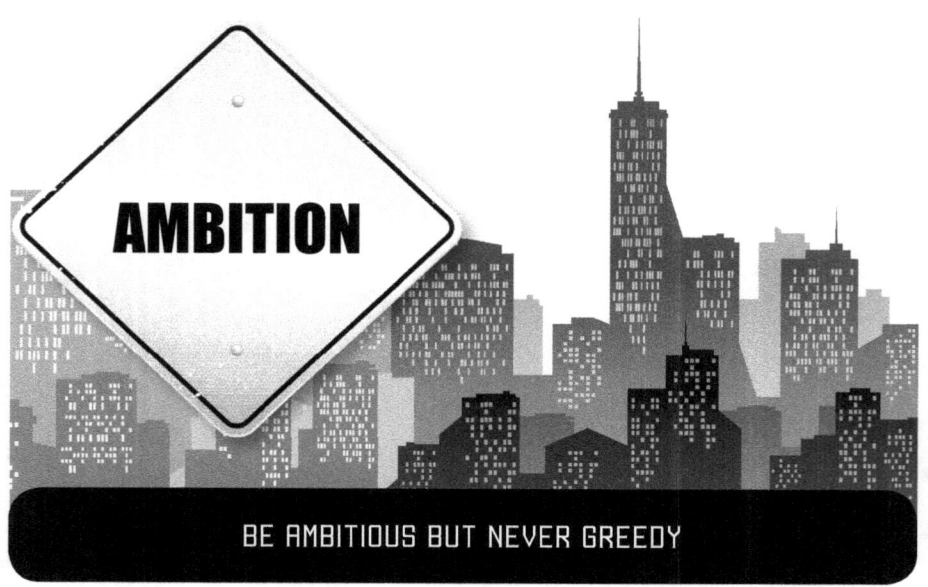

BE AMBITIOUS BUT NEVER GREEDY

*I*n order to achieve what you want in life, having ambition is necessary. Ambition means to have a strong desire to do or to achieve something. Possessing this quality will lead you to success. Young people need to have the desire and be ambitious in order to succeed. Some of the most important aspects about being successful involves spiritual things, and doing activities like sports, climbing a mountain or traveling, seeing the world, goals like learning a new language, a new trade, hobby, or even writing a book. Or maybe something as simple as trying to help as many needy people as you can. It may be collecting one million cans of food for the poor, volunteering one thousand hours of your time, touching lives in a positive way, reaching out to others, saving lives, earning a degree, finding a cure for a disease, or personal development like improving your health and staying fit.

Success does not always have to involve money or material items. It doesn't mean being greedy or over ambitious. Being ambitious means to have a strong desire and determination to succeed, and the intention to fulfill high and good aspirations.

DO EVERYTHING WITH ENTHUSIASM

Have enthusiasm for everything that you do whether it's school, work, recreation, church, family or friendships. Share your enthusiasm, excitement and interests. Don't be shy about showing your enthusiasm; let it be contagious! Enthusiasm means you have an intense enjoyment about something, and it is a necessary emotion to succeed. The outcome of your activities will be positive ones when you have eagerness. Something that characterizes young people is their ability to stay active, keep moving and the enthusiasm going!

Fill your life and do everything with enthusiasm, passion and joy. Add excitement and love to what you do, as well as faith and effort, because everything begins with you. Remember: If you can think it, you can achieve it; you just have to believe it. Success is not always winning: It often means going from failure to failure without losing an ounce of enthusiasm.

Enthusiasm and excitement should be regular ingredients in your relationships, education, and career. Lacking enthusiasm and excitement in your life is a hint that it is time to move on and make changes. Find what makes you happy and excites you, and keep the fire going.

"UPGRADE" YOURSELF

When we talk about upgrading, we generally think of a new phone or other electronic devices or even cars. What about upgrading things way more important like our life, education, knowledge, career, skills, performance, values, appearance, friendships and relationships?

As we grow as persons, we outgrow everything in life, so are you ready for an upgrade? From being a child and teenager to becoming a young adult, are you ready? This means you'll need to work on your personal growth, and grow mentally, emotionally, spiritually, and educationally.

Want to change the world? Begin by changing yourself. Work on self-improvement first and make a change now for the better. See the good things in life and look for the positive ones, not the negatives. Always strive to do your best. To become a better person, surround yourself with like-minded people, those who share your passion and vision, and who are positive and pleasant to be around. Find inspiration in positive people who encourage you and are on the same "frequency" as you. Surround yourself with smart individuals; however, if you are the smartest kid in the group, it's time to join a new group.

In order to improve ourselves you need to avoid negative people with negative thoughts, pessimistic individuals who are always complaining or whining about everything in life. Avoid persons who are on a different "frequency" level than you, who can be a bad influence in your life and are troublemakers. Run from people with no purpose in their life, who do not want to improve, since —as the saying goes— "If you lie down with dogs, you will get up with fleas." And another one goes: "You cannot soar like an eagle if you hang out with turkeys."

The sad reality sometimes is that some people choose to live a life of misery, otherwise they would try to change their situation. Most people are quite capable of making a change, but some refuse to do so. Our own reality should be very different.

To self-improve, we have to do whatever we can to better ourselves. Some people do nothing to better themselves and want or expect sympathy from others. This can also be like a contagious disease, so you need to get far away from individuals who live this way or you may be dragged down along with them. On the other hand, always try to help if you can, but just remember that you cannot help everyone all the time. It is impossible to help everybody, especially those who do not want help themselves or just refuse to change. Do not get caught up in their world in their web of problems.

Young man and woman, you are quite capable of helping yourself if you want to, and you are able to move up on your own. Self-improvement means you must be proactive and have motivation, without expecting others to do everything for you. Don't believe it is others' responsibility to help you improve because they may be better off than you are. There's another saying that goes: "Give a man a fish and you feed him for a day; teach a man to fish and you feed him for a lifetime." So learn to fish! Learn the skills you need to improve as an individual instead of wanting people to do the work for you.

Yes, sometimes we need to help our fellow human being to get back on their feet, but not support them for the rest of their lives because there are others who really need the help, and who cannot really help themselves. Here is where you need to focus your efforts and energy, on helping these folks. We all need a helping hand once in a while.

Never measure wealth just by material things, how much money you make, or how much money you have. Remember that health is also wealth. Always look for ways to progress. It does not matter how good you assume you are, there is always room for improvement. And, you need to ask yourself where you want to be tomorrow, next week, next month, and next year. So, what is self-improvement? Making yourself become a better person through your own personal abilities and efforts.

FIND YOUR STRENGTHS AND ROLE

With determination everything is possible. You need this very important quality if you are serious about your success. Success requires determination in order to conquer your goals. Determination means staying firm in your beliefs, sticking to your purpose, and staying in control of the situation.

Determination also helps you to see challenges through and not stop halfway. With determination you also stay in control of your life, course and destiny.

Often we give up too easy. We give up on our dreams because of the difficulties we encounter, but we will never know until we try. With this in mind, keep at it until you reach your dreams, goals and destination. Determination also means that no matter how difficult things become, you continue on; therefore, be persistent, don't give up easily, and work toward your goals without allowing anything or anyone to get in the way of your dreams, or discouraging you thus throwing you off course. Determination involves persevering, carrying on, hanging in there, and never giving up.

What else is determination? Reaching deep within you to find your strengths and your role, and being confident. Remember: What may seem ridiculous today, will not seem so ridiculous tomorrow. If people criticize you for your "crazy" ideas... Be proud! It means you are on to something big, and you may be way ahead of your time. All great achievers in human history were criticized at one time or another for their "crazy" ideas, or for trying something new, taking a different route, or for trying the unthinkable, achieving at the end what everyone said was not possible. Determination makes the difference. Fortune lies in your hands, and your habits will decide your future.

Determination means you weather the storm while continuing to move forward, regardless of your surrounding circumstances or conditions; you keep trying. There will never be a perfect moment to act, only the right circumstances; you make it perfect. If you are determined to achieve something then you'll persist, and as a result you will succeed. The moment we lose this determination and we stop doing things is the day we die.

Do you want to achieve something? Be insistent, persistent, and persevere; do not give up until you get it. That's determination.

Whatever you want to be you can be, but be prepared, look for opportunities, because opportunities will not come around looking for you. When you are just sitting at home playing video games or watching television for hours, texting your friends on your phone or spending hours on our favorite social media site, you are wasting valuable time; and, guess what? You are not going to arrive where you want to go. Sitting at home will get you nowhere; you have to get up and get out and look for opportunities. Opportunities abound, but you need to know where to look. Life is full of opportunities, just open your eyes and look around. If you don't see opportunities, then you create them. In order to do this, you'll need determination.

ACHIEVEMENT
YOU HAVE TO WANT IT

*A*chieving is working to make things happen, accomplishing something successfully. Life is measured by achievements, personal achievements. Children and young people often dream about what they want to be when they grow up. Haven't you?

As a young person, answering the following questions can help you get a sense of direction to where you want to go in life:

- What do you hope to achieve?

- What is your objective?

- Is there something to be achieved by your efforts?

- What are your goals and intentions?

- What will help you achieve these goals?

- How long will it take to reach your achievements?

- Will you need assistance, if so from whom and how?

- Are you putting in enough effort in developing the skills you will need to accomplish your purposes and aspirations?

- Do you want to earn a college degree?

- Do you want to live in a new city you like?

- Become a well-known performer or artist?

To achieve something in your life, you first need to decide and know what you want, and really want it. You need to desire it and be hungry for it, as well as maintain your goals in sight. Focus and visualize your goals in your mind, feel them, experience them and enjoy them.

Young people need to go through life knowing what they want and the direction they are headed. Knowing what you want is actually an achievement in itself. Teachers, counselors, successful peers and good role models, as well as career and occupational information, are all great resources to begin developing your goals. You will need to have courage to face possible obstacles along the way.

To achieve your goals you also need to concentrate and be attentive to what is really important. Avoid distractions and do not pay attention to things like media hype, since the media tends to exaggerate things for the sake of high ratings. But you need to also be careful with social media, since it has become one of the biggest distractions and time wasters. How much time are you spending on Facebook, Instagram or Snapchat? Instead try watching, listening and reading information that have the power to inspire and encourage you. Paying too much attention to negative news about the economy, politics or entertainment and celebrity gossip —or even about your friends— can drain your energy and waste your time. Some people actually use bad news as an excuse for their failures or to justify why they are not obtaining their success or reaching their full potential. Some kids, for example, blame peer pressure for doing what they do or for not doing what they should. Others blame their teachers for failing grades, or the economy for not having a job. Stay away from that way of thinking. Therefore, failure is not an option if you want to be effective and achieve success. After all, aren't you working toward achieving something great in your life?

GIVE YOUR ALL UNTIL IT HURTS

A popular book maintains the following: To achieve a high level of excellence in any field it takes 10,000 hours to master your skills and excel. To succeed in anything in life you need to invest 10,000 hours, that is 10 years of your time. That is 1000 hours a year, 83 hours a month, 3 hours a day. There are no shortcuts: 10,000 hours of dedication to reach your goal, your dream, and to succeed.

This talks about human potential, and potential in this case means a person has or shows the capacity to become or develop into something he or she wants in the future. Potential also refers to latent qualities or abilities that you have and that you must develop in order to accomplish a future success. Ask yourself the following questions:

- Have I put my full potential to work?

- Do I still have more to offer? Are there other resources within me that I haven't yet tapped into?

- Am I exploiting all my talents?

- Is there something in me that I haven't yet discovered?

- Are there other natural strengths or powers within me, and am I still developing my talents?

- Am I putting all my energy into my efforts?

Remember to give your all until it hurts, your energy and efforts into everything you do. Make an inventory of you skills and talents, and then think about how and where you can apply them. Discover and put to work your full potential.

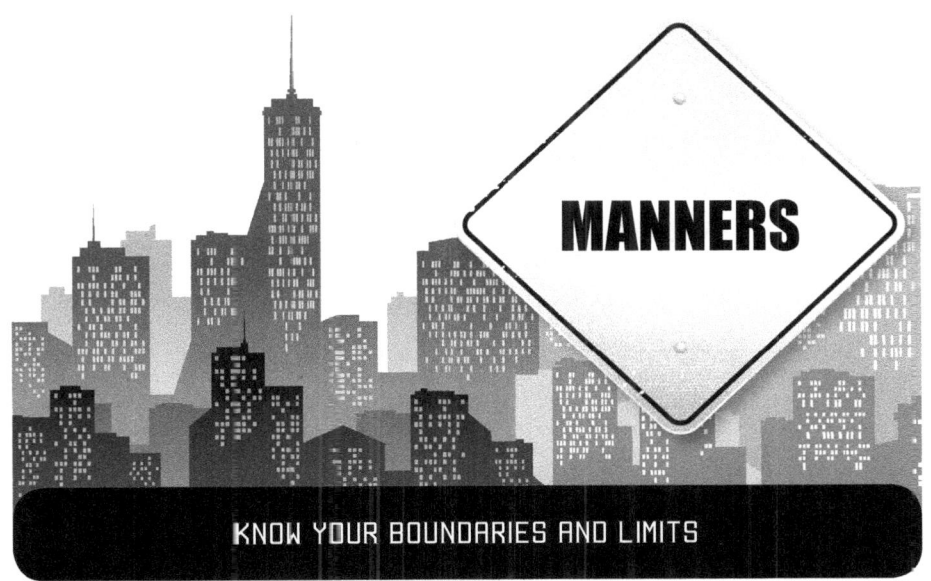

KNOW YOUR BOUNDARIES AND LIMITS

*P*ractice good manners. Showing good manners mean you have a polite or well-bred social behavior. Practice will not make you perfect, but will make you better.

How often do you use these magical words: "please" and "thank you?" Having good manners means you display acceptable conduct and social behavior, behave well in public and in private, follow the rules of conduct and have respect for others and their property. It also means you have self-respect, obey the rules, follow protocol, and exhibit proper etiquette. Good manners show you are mindful of others, use proper language and do not trespass upon others, insult, or offend them, that you do not take what does not belong to you, damage or destroy private property, and that when you borrow something you return it when you said you would or when they ask for it. You do not lie or cheat others, mislead or steal from them.

If you have good social skills, do not take advantage of people or their situation, but share and help out, show your manners. Being honest, humble, and never forgetting to say "thank you" or "you're welcome" are more examples of this. Or saying "I'm sorry," "forgive me" or "excuse me." Do you enjoy hearing people say "good morning," "good afternoon" or "good evening" to you? Most people would like to hear those words from you too. Do you hold the door open for someone, let others go in front of you, take turns, and share? Good manners mean you are nice and kind to people, not mean or rude. Are you polite and use manners when talking on the phone? Do you avoid *texting* at the dinner table, at the theater, at sporting events, or even when someone is serving you? How about when you text on your phone? Do you use nice and funny *emojis*? Being polite and displaying good manners will open doors for you, while bad manners will get doors slammed in your face. A simple "hello" or "how are you" can open many doors and bring you new opportunities and new friends.

Businesses know that one of the most important rules in life is good manners, therefore they spend millions in training their employees on how to be nice and kind to their customers. If you work at a fast-food restaurant or retail store, your job can depend on having or not having good manners. If you are just now learning proper manners, welcome to a new life of opportunities. Practice manners and you will succeed in all things you pursue.

Try helping a stranger out for no apparent reason; smile at everyone you meet; keep a positive attitude; start a conversation with a total stranger; initiate with a smile, a compliment, or a question. Life is a reflection of you, so going around with a negative attitude or being rude to others will in turn get you negative attitudes and results. An example of this is, if you kick a dog the animal will attack or bite you, but it you feed it and are kind, you will have a loyal friend for life.

If you feel you have been doing everything wrong, it's not too late to start over! But do not wait until tomorrow to make a change. Do not wait until you hit bottom to start having good manners. Begin now, this instant; make a resolution and stick to it. You will be amazed at how many opportunities will present themselves; how many doors will open for you, and how many new friends you will make. Everything in life is there for the taking.

One of the most fundamental manners is respect. Respect is the key; it is the main ingredient in the life potion. Remember to always practice respect and everything else will fall into place. Walk slowly, carry lots of respect, and never lose it. It all begins with respect, and it starts with you, the way that you respect yourself and others, your parents, teachers, elders, fellow students, coaches, teammates, counselors, the school's principal and your school. You have to give respect to earn respect. Remember to respect others so others can respect you; respect others' religions, race, beliefs, customs, dress codes, ideas, and opinions. Respect the environment and all living species. The way you conduct yourself is the way you will be treated. If you behave childish, you will be treated like a child. If you act disrespectful, you will be treated with disrespect. When listening to your music tone it down, when you speak do not yell; when in public respect others' space, don't touch others without their consent, and don't touch their belongings. If you are employed, respect your job, boss, fellow coworkers and company policies. Be respectful of your neighbors and other peoples' decisions —even if you don't agree with them. When driving a vehicle respect other drivers, the road, traffic signs and laws. Respect your country and flag. Always set your differences aside and respect other people.

Do not accuse anyone of anything without proof, because once respect is lost, all is lost. If respect is lost, problems will surely follow. Always watch your language, avoid being vulgar, yelling or screaming in public. Stay away from using insulting, hurtful or humiliating words. Respect means being considerate of others, taking others into account, giving them their space or not invading their privacy, and acknowledging them. Some individuals are under the false pretense they will earn respect by being disrespectful, but this is false, it is a myth. Disrespect will only get you ignored and turned away, so you need to be respectful; know your boundaries, do not cross that line, and know your limits. Remember if you do not respect yourself nobody else will.

Do not judge others based on ignorance simply because they do not agree with you, or they do not look like you, share your culture or tastes, or because they are not at the same social or economic level as you. The second you lose respect for others you also lose respect for yourself; disrespectful people live very lonely lives. Nobody will want to be around you if you are disrespectful. In life we reap what we sow; life is a reflection of you and your actions; if you want respect you need to give respect. If you are not receiving the respect you feel you deserve, it is probably because you have not earned it yet and need to work for it. Earn respect, appreciate honesty, gain trust, and return loyalty. Treat everyone with dignity and respect, this also includes you. Be proud of who you are and what you represent but do not fall into arrogance.

We often see people get hurt because they lose respect for what may seem simple, like the road and the road signs, which causes them to have an accident, or if they are riding a horse they lose respect for the beast and they fall and get hurt. If you lose respect for the mountain, you will fall and get hurt. If you lose respect for wild animals you can get hurt or worse, eaten alive. If you lose respect for the law you could end up in jail, the hospital or worse, the cemetery. Respect whatever it is you are doing. Respect everything around you. Respect is your responsibility.

Be courteous and polite to others, regardless of their social status. Show courtesy by allowing others to go in front of you, yielding to others in traffic, leaving someone your seat, your place, your parking space, your shopping cart, and while driving use the turn signal when changing lanes or turning. If you are late for an appointment or for work, call in to let them know you are running late. Your job does not need you; it's you who needs your job. Your school does not need you; again, you need your school. Show courtesy by letting others speak first and do not interrupt. Be courteous to your neighbors, your classmates, your teammates, school staff, and your family.

When you introduce yourself to someone, or when you are introduced to someone, you should always shake their hand. When you meet or greet someone, start with a warm friendly handshake (unless not permitted by their culture). A handshake should be as good as a contract. When you shake someone's hand, you need to look them in the eyes and give a firm handshake, not a "dead fish" shake; it should be an honest firm shake. Repeat their name to memorize it and show respect and interest. Also it is a good idea to smile as a friendly gesture, and do not forget to say a compliment. Always end a conversation with, "It was a pleasure meeting you." If you need to leave excuse yourself; remember everyone is important. You will not have a second opportunity to make a first impression.

When you arrive at a location or if someone arrives at your location, you should always acknowledge and greet them. Be friendly to all, shake everyone's hand if possible. When you greet customers, say "welcome"; when people visit you say "welcome." Also, a compliment is a good way to start a conversation. As a rule always be polite; end the greeting when they leave or you leave with "have a great day," "take care," "see you soon," "nice to see you," "come back to see us soon," and so forth.

Always acknowledge people as you approach them or as they approach you. Do not ignore anyone regardless of who they are, their age, race, condition, position, social status or occupation. Not acknowledging people is a sign of humiliation or lack of respect; you are basically demonstrating to them that you are better than they are or that you feel superior to them, or that you think they are inferior. Always avoid these bad manners; acknowledge all. Also acknowledge those that have succeeded, or risen above the rest. Give credit where credit is due, acknowledge those that have given of themselves, even when you feel you are wrong or have made a mistake. If you have a problem, acknowledge it and don't try to hide it. When you encounter others always acknowledge them.

Excuse yourself if you need to leave, if you are blocking someone's view or way, if you need something say, "excuse me," to get someone's attention, to ask a question, or if someone is talking and you need to interrupt say, "excuse me." Don't speak or answer if they are not speaking to you, or wait until they are done before you jump in. Also, it is very rude to walk in front of people or walk through the middle of a group, so before interrupting say, "excuse me." If you need to go through say, "Excuse me, may I go through?" Or, "I need to get through," and, if someone is invading your space say, "excuse me, may I help you?"

A magic word is *please*. The word please has loads of power; it's amazing how many things you can obtain by simply saying "please" when asking. Practice saying please. When you ask for something you should always say that magic word. When you need help or need a favor start with, "Please, can you do me a favor?" Or, "Please help me out," or, "Please, I need directions, I'm lost." When emailing someone and you need information, write: "Please, can you send me the information..." At the store say, "please" when asking for help or, "Please, may I have my change back?" In school say please to be excused, or please when having your teacher or peer explain a question if you did not understand it. When you want to be left alone, you can say something like: "Please do not bother me, I am working," or, "I am studying," or, "excuse me, but please don't touch my car," "please do not take my seat," and so on.

Never forget to say "thank you" or "I really appreciate it, thank you very much." We never seem to say thank you enough, we need to say it more often. Anytime someone does something for you do not forget to say "thank you." When someone offers you something, even if you decline say, "No thank you." Always say thank you to people that serve you, or yield to you, give you the right of way, help you out, give you directions or advice. If they open the door for you, allow you to go first, or are courteous to you say, "thank you." If someone did something for you regardless of what it is say, "thank you." Be thankful to God for what you have, for a new day and new opportunities, before meals say, "thank you," and before going to bed thank God for a great day. Never forget to thank people during your daily routine, and when someone thanks you, do not forget to say "you are very welcome."

Why do we find it so hard to say we are sorry? If we feel we did something wrong we need to learn to apologize and say we are sorry. If you feel you have hurt someone physically by accident or emotionally (there is never a reason to hurt someone on purpose), or if you feel you have offended someone, ask for forgiveness. When you do not understand something, don't be afraid to say, "I'm sorry, but I do not understand." If you cannot hear someone speaking just say, "I'm sorry, but I cannot hear you." If you feel you were disrespectful, apologize. If you interrupt when someone is speaking, apologize, or if you said something you did not mean simply apologize. If you bump into someone by accident, whether it is at school or in public, saying you are sorry and apologizing is not a sign of weakness, it is a sign of strength. Never be too proud to say you are sorry; if you feel you have failed someone just tell them you are sorry.

In order for us to find forgiveness we also need to learn how to forgive. To find closure we need to forgive and move on. We cannot go through life holding on to grudges and carrying a heavy load of hate our entire lives. You cannot carry this weight forever, and eventually you will break. Whether you have been insulted, assaulted or offended, you need to forgive and move on. Harboring hate will only destroy you, so just leave it all behind, forgive and start over again. Give yourself another opportunity by forgiving. You cannot ask for forgiveness if you are not yet capable of forgiving; if God forgives ours sins, we also need to be able to forgive.

Having good manners is something you'll need throughout your life, so beginning now as a young person will give you experience for the years to come.

RESPONSIBILITY

DOING THE RIGHT THING EVEN WHEN NOBODY IS WATCHING YOU

Responsibility is another key attribute for success. What does responsibility mean? It means you are where you are supposed to be, doing what you are supposed to be doing, and basically, that you don't need a baby-sitter. When you are a responsible young person you do things because you know it is your responsibility, and because you realize you are accountable, reliable, people can count on you, and you do the right thing even when nobody is watching you.

Always be responsible in everything you do: school, work, and in your community. Responsibility should include all aspects and actions in your life. Do not pass the buck. Be responsible with family and friends and property entrusted to you. When you are wrong, take full responsibility for your actions. If you have a problem, admit it; the first step to recovery is to admit you have a problem. You will always need to take responsibility for your actions.

Remember, with age, education, a job promotion and salary comes more responsibility. Being responsible means you are trustworthy to do what is expected of you, and always fulfilling your duties and obligations no matter what. You always need to come through and focus on doing what is right. If you do not take full responsibility for your actions, you will never grow as a person, you will never succeed. Being responsible, on the other hand, brings many benefits and opportunities for growth.

DON'T ALLOW THE WORLD TO CHANGE YOU. YOU CHANGE THE WORLD

Our attitude makes the difference in our lives. It is all in the attitude and how you look at life. The way you handle situations and your emotions, a positive attitude is one of the best attributes you can have. Never forget the power of positive thinking, beliefs and expectations so be mindful of what you say, what you think, and what you do. Have a positive view of life.

You can change your attitude, but to make changes you first need to change your behavior and your way of thinking. You need to learn how to handle your emotions and feelings, because sometimes you may get frustrated if you're not able to understand something, or if things are not going your way, or if you do not know how to handle a certain situation. At times, you might not know how to react to certain things, so you may start to develop an attitude in hopes of being left alone, but it's always best to stay positive and calm, analyze the situation, and stay in control.

Attitude is everything. Like the saying goes, where there's a will, there's a way. Maintain a positive attitude in your life and good things will happen. Surround yourself with positive individuals with good emotions and attitudes, and avoid those with negative attitudes. Like negative individuals who try to steal your positive energy, these people will only drain your energy. Remember, it's all in your attitude and how you look at things. It's all mental and the way you think, so be proud of who you are and what you represent; always maintain that positive attitude no matter what. Regardless of the situations or adversities you may face, it may not always be about you, so be tolerant and sensitive to others. Do not fear failure or what others may say since others will not come to feed you when you are hungry, or bail you out when you are in trouble. You need to look out for you.

Don't worry about things that are unimportant or that you cannot change, focus on what you can change, and don't allow the world to change you. You change the world. Take charge of your life, take control of the wheel, the direction and speed of your life, your journey, on your terms. Do not allow others to determine your identity, your future, or your plans. Do not change your plans for others or your attitude to fit theirs. Always be optimistic and look for the good in all things. Remember that words will open doors, but it is your actions that will carry you through. Always focus on leading and not following. Never allow others to use you for their purpose; avoid those who only want to benefit from you, and surround yourself with individuals who you will benefit from mutually. There needs to be a balance in everything to make it work, and never be fooled and pretend to be something you are not. You will only be fooling yourself, so do not get in over your head in things like financial debt just to impress others. Always try growing as a person and you will be able to overcome anything with the right attitude.

Having a positive attitude is a key ingredient for success. To prosper you need to be positive so think on prosperity, abundance, peace, harmony, happiness, laughter, love and joy. Have faith and good things will happen, and believe in you; with faith all things are possible, faith moves mountains.

The most powerful tool that you possess is your mind, which is more powerful than all the computers in the world combined, but you need to put it to work for you. And only you can do it, no one can do it for you. Make up your mind on what you want to do and go for it; do not let anything stop you. Your mind is also a muscle that needs to be exercised just like the rest of your body. Keep it in shape, exercise it. Put it to use. Everything originates in your mind.

Block all negative thoughts or ideas. Negative thinking will only result in negative outcomes. To reach your goals you need to believe and visualize them. Picture them in your mind, be positive. Have faith, it will come to you and be open to all possibilities; nothing is impossible. Whatever you think about will eventually materialize. You also need to block out negative feelings like anger or resentment. Remove them out of your mind, your life and your system. Fill your mind with positive ideas, things of joy and happiness.

A PURPOSE IN LIFE IS FUNDAMENTAL

What is your purpose in life? What are you meant to be or do? As a young person it is very important that you find your purpose. Each day you need to get out of bed with a purpose in mind. What is your aim today? What do you hope to accomplish today? Make a list of ten things you would like to accomplish during the day, and if you are able to accomplish seven things out of the ten, than you have succeeded. You'll be able to say it was a very productive, successful and meaningful day. What is your intention, purpose, goal, or target for today? Make sure that at the end of the day you have something to show for your efforts. Ask yourself: What is my target today? What am I looking for? What is the purpose for what I am going to do? Having a purpose in life is fundamental; living life without purpose is meaningless. Try to live a purpose-filled and meaningful life.

DISCIPLINE
LEARN TO FOLLOW THE RULES

*L*ike with everything else in life, we have to have discipline in order to succeed. You need to be disciplined, which means you follow the rules and laws, control your behavior and emotions, and learn to obey and follow orders. In a country of laws like the United States, either you discipline yourself or the government will do it for you, so make sure you stay in control of your conduct.

Discipline starts at home, so learn to follow the rules at this stage and you will be okay. Begin by respecting your parents and the rules they lay down for you in order to create good habits that will later help you succeed in life. Examples of these rules are doing your chores, respecting curfews, keeping your grades up at school, being truthful and respectful with all family members, eating healthy and not wasting food, just to name a few. Some of the most basic rules you learn as you grow up may seem boring or unpleasant, but as an adult you'll see the benefits these had in your forming years. Disregarding those rules have landed a lot of young people in all sorts of trouble, and in some cases even ruined their lives.

Discipline is not only important in your personal and family circles. Society also imposes even more strict rules on us to create a safe and productive environment for all. Collective rules demand that we behave appropriately at school, work and public places. This includes respecting all people and their property. Individual discipline is also important. This includes respecting yourself, staying strong and healthy by not using drugs, alcohol, or smoking, not getting into a relationship until you are 18 years of age, protecting your image, staying safe and so forth.

When you are disciplined the positive results will be evident in your life, your education and career. Have a set of personal rules to live by. Be neat and thorough with your work, your school assignments, or whatever you do in life; do not settle for mediocrity. Remember, a clean life runs smoother. Keep your work area clean, neat and organized. Cleanliness is very important in all areas of your life. Whether it's your work area, your office, your room, your life in general, maintain a clean appearance. It is your life and your image, so take care of it, stay focused and do one thing at a time. Focus on your goals, be persistent, and push yourself to the limit. See for yourself how cool and positive it is to have discipline in your life.

GET EXCITED ABOUT WHAT YOU ARE DOING!

Whatever we do in life, we need to have and retain motivation. To do this we first need to find out what motivates us and moves us, the general desire to do something, as well as the reasons we have for acting or behaving in a particular way.

Some ways to get motivated include learning about motivational and personal growth by reading books, watching videos or downloading motivational mobile apps on our smart phones. As a young person, make sure you also belong to groups who organize or attend inspiring events geared for young people. Some young men and women return from these events or trips not only motivated but with a vision to change their world. Then you can begin to motivate and share your enthusiasm with those around you. Once you are motivated you'll want to avoid negative individuals who don't share your beliefs, dreams, and your vision. But through motivation you can influence others and show them how they can also benefit. Be the driving force.

Motivation, in other words, is loving what you do. If you do not love what you are doing, then make a change, do something different to find your passion. It is not always about money, it is about being satisfied with what you are doing, and where life is taking you. A person may prefer to be a nurse than a doctor, although doctors earn more money, because working with patients as a nurse will give this individual more fulfillment. In order to stay motivated, sometimes you need to visualize the end result, the trophy you'll win. Keep your eyes on the prize.

Excitement is fundamental, so get excited about what you are doing! However, when channeled in a positive way, anxiety and pressure can also work as motivators, because they may force you to act and make decisions, as well as influence and inspire your peers. Don't let obstacles stand in the way of your objective and goals. Be thankful for obstacles, for the challenges life throws at you, for this builds character and determines who you really are and what you will become. Don't let anyone or anything discourage you from reaching your goals. If someone tells you this or that, or that it is too hard, just let them know and see through your dedication and determination. Do not change your plans or pretend to be something you are not just to please others. Motivate others in a positive way. In order to be the driving force you need the ability to encourage others to follow.

To begin and achieve your goals you need to have and maintain personal motivation, self-confidence, and faith in yourself. If you tried something and did not succeed it was probably because you did not want it bad enough. If you want it and have faith you will acquire it. Faith will not make things easier, but it will make things possible. Remember, to succeed in anything you need to have the desire and motivation; it is that need or desire that energizes and guides behavior.

VICTORY WITHOUT STRUGGLE IS NO VICTORY AT ALL

*R*esiliency lies in the human ability to get up after every fall. To succeed in life, we need to have the power to bounce back time after time, and be able to recover, regroup and make another stride until we get through. To be resilient means you are able to recover quickly from a disruptive change or misfortune in your life. Imagine a three-dimensional (3-D) object that after being bent, compressed or stretched out of shape it comes back to its original state. If you suffer a loss or mess up, get up, pick up the pieces, regroup and move on; no use crying over spilled milk. The quote attributed to a German philosopher, "That which does not kill us, makes us stronger," means if you are determined you will emerge wiser and stronger after you experience a crisis. There is nothing you cannot overcome; you will survive. Victory without struggle is no victory at all.

EXPERIENCES AND NOT FAILURES

*A*s humans we all make mistakes. Some mistakes cause some loss in our lives, while others end up being beneficial if we learn from them. Mistakes are a critical part of the learning process. As a young person, the most important thing you can do about personal mistakes is to learn from them, and not make the same mistakes twice; think of them as experiences, not failures. Feeling excessively sorry over a mistake and for too long is not going to revert a mistake. The world is not going to end just because a mistake was made; get over it, get up, carry on, analyze the results and what went wrong. Learn and move on. As human beings we learn by trial and error; we live and learn. If it wouldn't be for mistakes we would not be here.

Nevertheless, our emphasis should be in avoiding making mistakes as much as we can, and in doing things right. A study from the University of Exeter showed that our brain prevents us from repeating the same mistake by giving us an *'early warning signal'*. Psychologists identified a mechanism in the brain that reacts in just 0.1 seconds to things that have caused us to make errors in the past. So be attentive to that early warning signal!

HARMONY

MAKING EVERYTHING FIT INTO PLACE

*A*lways do your very best to live in harmony with nature, your fellow human being, and the environment. Maintain that harmony throughout your life with everything that surrounds you, peace, and positive vibes. Make everything fit into place like a perfect puzzle, just like God intended it to be. Everything has its place in life.

THE WORLD IS JUST A REFLECTION OF YOU

Happiness is a way of life, a choice. Happiness lives inside us, it's a personal feeling. If we cannot make ourselves happy then nobody else can. Happiness does not depend on what surrounds us, but what is inside. We decide in the morning that it's going to be a great day. When you get up out of bed say, "I am so happy," and stay happy throughout the day. Have happy thoughts and positive feelings, and smile. Leave no room for other thoughts; focus on joy, happiness, prosperity, perfection, abundance, comfort, peace and harmony.

Do what makes you happy because you hold the key to your own happiness, no one else does, and don't give that key to someone else. Some people say, "I am going to find someone to make me happy," but this is a total myth. If that person who is supposed to be the reason for your happiness leaves, you will be very unhappy. Instead you need to find someone to share in your happiness. Do not base your happiness on material things either, since that can be lost along with your happiness. Your surroundings should not determine your happiness; it is what is inside of you that determines it. You can be happy right here and right now. Doing what you are doing, nothing else matters.

Smile at the world and the world will smile back. What you see is what you get because the world is just a reflection of you, your thoughts and feelings, so be happy. Treat everybody with a smile and this will come back to you and will open doors for you. If you treat people well and with a smile you will always receive better treatment. Always treat others the way you want to be treated. You can make yourself feel better just by smiling. Practice smiling in front of the mirror and in public and you will see the change in you and other people's faces; a smile is very contagious. Being happy and treating everyone with a smile will open up new opportunities for you, so do not be afraid to express your happiness with a big smile. Smiles and laughter cure all of life's ills.

Always try to be in a good mood and smiling. Be courteous and friendly and you will be treated well. If you are in a bad mood or are rude to others, then others will be rude to you, people will avoid and stay away from you. Rude people live very lonely lives; remember you will attract whatever it is you portray. So smile and be happy.

LISTEN TO INSPIRATIONAL MUSIC

Music is a very important part of our lives. As a young person you likely spend a good amount of time listening to music, and have your own share of favorite bands and singers. Music can produce constructive or destructive thoughts in our minds and its influence is very strong, therefore be careful of the music you listen to.

Try listening to music that promotes family values, peace, harmony, hope, unity, diversity, tolerance, and positive messages. Listen to spiritual music that soothes you and gives you a sense of peace and joy, one that inspires you and motivates you through its lyrics. Do not get caught up listening to music that promotes or glorifies violence, drugs, alcohol, sex, easy money or false riches, or encourages hate and racism, persecution, discrimination, fancy jewelry or cars, gang violence or violence in general against women or others. Do not try to imitate the message of this type of music or fall prey to its false message.

DEFINE YOUR CORE VALUES

Core values are guiding principles that dictate our behavior and actions. They help us to know what is right from wrong, and to find out if we are on the right path to fulfill our goals.

Core values can be *internal* or *external*. Internal core values are principles, standards and rules to live by. They are similar to a guiding light and compass to lead you in the right direction. These values will determine what is important in your life, how you conduct yourself, your behavior, and what you stand for. They will give your life purpose and meaning.

Integrity, ethics, faith, spirituality, respect, responsibility, trust, honesty, self-discipline, wisdom, fairness, family, friendships, forgiveness and freedom, are just a few examples of your internal values. What does your list of internal values look like? What do you already have and what do you need to add? Make your own list by order of importance in your life.

External core values are expectations you value the most and aim to accomplish. These typically include earning a college education, developing a professional career, good health and fitness, personal success, financial independence and many others. The list can be endless; make sure you also make one to establish your external core values.

An example of external core values in your list could be education, but once you obtain your degree, does your family become your number one priority or your career? Professional success can bring prosperity to you and your family. Career and family are both good values, but if your most important value is to achieve professional success, your family may become second and end up being neglected. This is where your priorities come into action. If the wellbeing of your family is your number one external value, your career most likely will be successful since your end goal is your family's happiness.

Distribute your time and energy on areas in the order of importance, most meaningful and that are most significant to you; everything else takes second place. This will help you prioritize your life and keep you focused.

Establishing your internal and external core values is one of the most important steps you have to give early in life. So, are you ready to make your lists?

DOING THE RIGHT THING

When a person is honest and has strong moral values he or she has integrity. Integrity means doing the right thing and playing by the rules, even when no one is watching. Be faithful to your cause, stay honest, and keep high moral values. Integrity is a fundamental human quality that demonstrates the type of character you have, that you are trustworthy.

Young man, young woman, stay true to your word, and never compromise your principles. Always follow good ethics, do what is right even when you have to go against the majority, and when you are singled out or criticized because you defend your values, what you stand for and believe in. Stick to your moral principles no matter what and protect your values. Defend what you believe in, what is right and just. If you make promises fulfill them; be a person of principles.

Never allow yourself to be corrupted, do not be tempted with illegal activity or immoral offers. Do not sacrifice your integrity or lower your standards for the sake of others or for profit or popularity because you will lose more than gain in the end. Standards are principles of conduct we should follow. As a young person you should always keep high standards in every aspect of your life and never compromise them. Do not be afraid to raise the bar, meet or exceed your and others' expectations. Keep a high level of quality in all you do. Never lower your standards just to please others or fit in. Take care of your reputation and your integrity because once you lose them you may never gain them back. People and companies have been ruined by a bad reputation, but those who have integrity are highly regarded and respected, and enjoy the true rewards of trustworthiness.

WORK ETHIC

TAKE YOUR JOB SERIOUSLY

Some young people begin working to gain experience and earn some money while they are still attending high school. Perhaps you are already working or planning to get a job. However, it is very important that you do not lose sight of your education if you get a job. For youth, education should always come first.

Both as a student and an employee, you must always maintain a good work ethic by being thorough and neat. Conduct yourself in a professional manner, be committed, responsible, reliable, punctual, and always work hard and do your best. Do not rely on others to supervise your work or check it all the time. Double check your own work before you turn it in. Do your very best and give one hundred ten percent. Do what is right and practice good work habits. Take your job seriously, and when you make a mistake or feel you are wrong, simply admit it and don't try to hide it or blame it on someone else. This is how you grow and earn respect as a person. Support your boss, your company, for if the company succeeds, so will you. Same goes for your team or crew.

To make it big in life you have to think big, you have to work hard and pay your dues with sweat and tears, scratches and blisters, and by dedication and sacrifice. All this will pay dividends down the road; it's like a bank account, a savings where you have to deposit before you can withdraw. So the more you deposit the greater the return with interest; that's what life is about. Farmers work the land, plant the seed, and then reap the harvest; you should see your work in a similar way. Take into account that you cannot withdraw what you have not deposited. You cannot harvest what you have not sowed. It's just common sense. Of course, this process takes time, hard work and dedication; it will not happen overnight, but if you want it bad enough and are willing to work hard, it will happen. You will enjoy the fruits of your harvest.

But let's talk about work ethic. Good work ethic means you do your job even when your boss is not watching. Do not wait for your boss to tell you what to do, just do it. And when you are finished find something else to work on. Do not sit around after you finish a task; this is not good work ethic, especially when your boss is present and customers are waiting. Keep in mind, you get paid for eight hours of work, therefore, your boss expects eight hours of work not four or six. And also remember that usually your next job depends on the present one, as a potential employer may contact your last employer to ask about you for a reference. Stay busy at all times, do not waste time sitting around or goofing off; this is a sure way to get fired. Being fired from a job may hurt you for a while. Your present job is important in order to build a strong resume for future employment.

Be responsible with your employer and your work duties. Good work ethic means you are committed to your company's vision, your coworkers, clients, and your cause. Do not cut corners at the cost of quality or service. Strive to deliver quality day in and day out. Take care of customers' needs first; your job depends on it. Always ensure customers leave happy; if they leave upset they will not return, they will go somewhere else, and take their money and even other customers with them. Customers do not need you or your bad attitude; you need your customers. Always aim to please, quality does not take a day off. Remember the best advertisement is word of mouth, referrals, so woo your customers. Do not be afraid to go the extra mile. Aim to please.

TAKE CARE OF YOURSELF

Your physical and mental health always come first. Health is wealth, so always take care of your health and yourself first. Stay healthy by making healthy choices and eating nutritious meals. Always choose healthy activities, exercise regularly, get enough sleep, and practice meditation or yoga. Stay away from drugs, alcohol, tobacco, and avoid hazardous activities. Staying healthy includes having healthy friendships and surroundings.

Never sacrifice your health in exchange for success. Remember the phrase by Eubie Blake, who lived to be 96, "If I'd known I was going to live this long, I'd have taken better care of myself." Well the time is now to begin taking better care of yourself. You can live that long and longer, but take care of yourself first. Health comes before money and material luxuries. Money cannot buy your health, time, or bring back loved ones.

HUMILITY

ALWAYS KNOW THAT WE ARE ALL EQUAL

*I*n a world plagued by arrogance and self-importance, humility will make you stand out in the crowd. Always be and stay humble, and do not try to be something that you are not. Be proud of who you are and of your talents and accomplishments, but not to the point of arrogance. Reach for the stars but keep your feet on the ground. Remember that humbleness will bring opportunities, while arrogance will get you nowhere. Never pretend to know more than what you really know or to have more than what you actually have. Never be too proud to admit your faults or ask for help if you have a problem. Always know that we are all equal. Listen to other point of views; everyone has the right to express themselves, even if you do not agree. Accept yourself as you are and never pretend to be perfect.

ACCEPTANCE

GOD MADE YOU THE WAY YOU ARE FOR A REASON

*L*earn to accept others as they are, regardless of race, religion, social status, beliefs or customs. Promote diversity, celebrate life, look for the positive in people, and do not focus on people's negative sides. The reasons we become disappointed in people are because we look for defects, flaws, and we place too much focus on their negatives, rather than their positives and their qualities; learn to accept the things in life you cannot change.

Too many people spend thousands or tens of thousands of dollars — even millions— in changing their appearance, to the point where they look like a total different person. The late pop singer Michael Jackson is a good example. He actually destroyed his appearance with one hundred cosmetic operations.

Accept and love yourself as you are, and do not compare yourself to others. Comparing yourself to your peers blurs your vision and keeps you from seeing how blessed you are. Focus on your qualities and not on your flaws; you are beautiful and you do not need a mirror or others' opinions to confirm it. Say, "I am beautiful and I am mine, and nobody can take my beauty away." Accept yourself the way you are, the way God created you. God made you the way you are for a reason; you are special, with specific talents, and He has a plan for you.

*B*enevolence is a desire to do good for others. Never miss an opportunity to help a person in need, share. It's a blessing to be able to help. Think about a time when a person shared something with you, and try to remember how this made you feel.

You can share your knowledge, time, and resources. Being in a position to be able to share and help is a blessing and a privilege. As a young person you may not have plenty of resources yet to share, but you'll reach a stage in your life where you can share more.

Lend a hand to others by sharing of yourself, volunteering your time, sharing your resources and the fruit of your harvest. Share your space, your transportation, and remember, when God blesses you with riches it is meant to be shared with others.

Donate your most precious resource: your time. Volunteer, give to a good cause, or donate some of your possessions to a special cause or nonprofit organization. When you give or donate, do it from the heart and without expecting anything in return. We need to be generous with our money. God has blessed you to help others, and not for you to fill your life with toys, luxuries or more material things than what you need, especially while others go hungry or without having their basic needs. Expect nothing in return, and you will never be disappointed. It is always better to give than to receive.

Show compassion and caring for others. Compassion means to be concerned for the sufferings or misfortunes of others. Always be concerned for others' wellbeing. Be sympathetic to their needs, misfortunes, suffering, hunger, pain; this includes other living creatures as well, not just humans. Sometimes you may think you have it bad, but some have it worse. If we only knew what others are going through, we would be more compassionate.

We all need a helping hand at one time or another. Helping means to make it easier for a person to do something by offering our services or resources. We always need to do our best to help others, but before we do, we need to help ourselves. This means you need to be in an able position to help others.

Before deciding to step in and help, examine the situation and help those that really need help and are not just using you. Help those who are in real need. You may sometimes feel sorry and sympathetic for people, but keep in mind that some individuals like living a certain way, and others just like to whine and cry about everything but do nothing to change their situation. If they choose to live this way they do not really need the help; get far away from these folks. If you have ever flown by plane, this may remind you of when the flight attendant goes through the emergency procedures before the plane takes off: "... in case of an emergency put on your oxygen mask first before helping others..." So help yourself first in order to help others.

You know others will need your help so be prepared to give them a hand. Help the needy, the sick, the hungry, and those that cannot help themselves. When you help do it without expecting anything in return. In the same way, never be afraid to ask for help when you need it, and never be too proud to ask.

Care for the ones who can't be heard, the abandoned, the neglected, the homeless, the depressed, and the ones who have lost hope. Work on giving them hope and restore their faith. Show that you care, that you are there for them, that you will never leave them, and ensure them things will be okay. Take time to help and console and comfort the less fortunate.

And finally, sometimes we all need a little encouragement to carry on, to continue fighting and not give up. Giving encouragement means we are giving someone support, confidence, or hope. Encourage others to improve their lives, show them support, and give them confidence to carry on and not give up hope. Many times we just need a little encouragement, a little support and a little push. A few words of encouragement go a long way.

GRATEFULNESS

THINK ABOUT HOW BLESSED YOU ARE

Gratefulness is one of the human qualities people value the most. Being grateful simply means being appreciative of the benefits we have received from others.

Be grateful for what you have and for the people you have in your life like your parents and teachers, and for everything they do for you. Often we do not know what we have until it is gone, so do not wait until then to thank them. Show how much you appreciate all they do for you by being grateful for what you have; even though you may not always get what you want, you will always get what you need.

Be thankful and grateful for a new day, for others and their friendship. Far worst things happen around the world like people dying of hunger or disease or stricken by poverty, violence, persecution, or injustices; such things are happening right now as you are reading this book. Sometimes we tend to get upset just because someone scratched our car, or a bird just pooped on the hood, or someone took our parking space, or stole our shopping cart. Think about how blessed you are; there are people so much happier than us with much less than what we have.

Here is a story that can exemplify gratefulness: One day a man saw his next door neighbor, who was always raking leaves off the ground from his trees. The man asked his neighbor if he ever got tired of always raking up leaves from his "messy trees." The neighbor's only response was: "Actually no. As a matter of fact I love it, because it is a sign from God that I am alive, that I am still healthy enough and able to rake up leaves, and for this I am very grateful." The man was only able to see the dry leaves and what seemed to be a tedious, boring task; his neighbor, instead, saw the bigger picture, one where he could see all the precious things he was thankful for.

Make a list of all the people and things you can be grateful for. Go back to your early memories, and begin thinking about the times when your parents, siblings, teachers and friends did something for you. Take an opportunity to thank them, and tell them why you are grateful for them.

CHOOSE YOUR FRIENDS WISELY

We need to value our friends because they are people who enrich our lives. We all need each other to survive. We need company because loneliness can kill; we need the warmth and protection of others. So it's important that you make friends, and do your best to keep them.

Use wisdom to choose the people you'll call friends. Keep this in mind when choosing friends, and ask yourself: Does this person really like me for who I am or only for what I have to offer? Determine if the people you have in mind to be friends with, love you for who you are or if they just need you. Will you be their stepping stone, their lifeline, their bank, or their go-to-guy? Could you trust a certain individual with your life if you were in a dangerous place or situation? Would that person abandon you or stick with you through thick and thin? Would you trust this person with your life, or would you need to watch your back?"

Be careful with those "friends" who only want to use you and benefit from you, who seem like they are always asking for one thing or another. Whether it is money, a ride because you have a car, or those "friends" who only hang out when you have money to buy them things. These type of friends are also called leaches or fake friends. Be careful with these so-called friends because the minute you have nothing to offer they will abandon you. They are easy to recognize because they always want you to do favors for them, but they do not respond as well when you need a favor. Sometimes it is wise to test them, see if they would do the same for you. In business relationships or partnerships, the conditions are no different. There has to be equality and balance in order to succeed. You give and take, and everyone contributes equally so if the scale tips to one side it all falls apart.

Look for those special qualities you want in a friendship in people you meet. A real friend should possess at least some of these qualities: respectful, trustworthy, honest, dependable, loyal, empathic, non-judgmental, and good listener. Needless to say, you should also possess these qualities. Seek individuals who are like-minded, equally-yoked, who share similar beliefs and outlook on life and people who enjoy the same sports, outings, hobbies, and so forth.

PUNCTUALITY

NEVER MAKE OTHERS WAIT FOR YOU

When you complete a required task or fulfill an obligation before or at a previously designated time, you are being punctual. Strive to always arrive early to your appointments whether it is work, school, or personal meetings. Allow enough time to arrive as scheduled. This usually means you have to prepare ahead of time, even a day before. You are responsible for ensuring that you arrive on time, so make arrangements in terms of personal grooming and transportation ahead of time. Never make people wait for you; it is very unprofessional to arrive late to meetings or to keep people waiting. Encourage others to be punctual as well. Punctuality speaks volumes about what we portray, our persona and our character.

ALL THE MONEY IN THE WORLD CANNOT BUY YOU TIME

Time is an irreplaceable gift, so take full advantage of it. Work on those things that matter. Invest your time on things that will move you forward and closer to achieving your goals and objectives. Time is our most precious resource because we cannot recover it. All the money in the world cannot buy you time or stop time. Therefore, use your time wisely.

Make time for family and friends. Make time to improve and maintain optimal health because money cannot buy it. Do not hang around with people who only waste your time. Use time on productive things for your life. Money cannot buy time, but time is money, so look for ways, ideas, and better routes to improve your life.

Time is a most precious resource. You can recover almost anything in life, except time. Once time has passed, you cannot bring it back.

TIME FRAMES

HELPING YOU STAY ON TRACK

A time frame is a period of time used or planned for a particular action or project. What are your time frames? How long should it take for you to complete a task or a job? Have set time frames for everything you do. Time yourself, keep track of time, and try to improve your time by making the most out of it. Make each second, each minute, and each day count.

Time frames are necessary for everything. They give you a sense of where you want or expect to be in one or six months, or even a year from now. All dreams, goals, and objectives need to have time frames. They help you measure your progress. For example: "By sixteen, I want to have my driver's license and have a part-time job for my expenses and independence." Or, "By the time I'm eighteen, I want to be in college and have my own car." Hold yourself accountable and ensure you stay within your allotted time frames. Time frames will help you stay on track to reach your goals.

YESTERDAY IS GONE. TODAY IS REALITY. TOMORROW IS A DREAM

Make the best of every single day. Make every day count. Always do things with a sense of urgency and do not procrastinate. Do not leave for tomorrow what you should do today; tomorrow may never arrive, or tomorrow other problems may present themselves.

Take care of situations as they present themselves and do not let things pile up. Life is short, your future is now. Whether it is work or play, do things with a sense of urgency because time is money and sometimes we have neither. This does not mean that you rush into things carelessly. Remember yesterday is gone, today is reality, tomorrow is a dream.

THINK TWICE BEFORE YOU MAKE A CHOICE

*A*s we get older and enter our teenage years, life starts to get real, and we come to realize it is time to take life more serious. We arrive at a point in time when we need to recognize it is time to grow up and begin acting our age.

If you are reading this book, chances are you are a young person who wants to take charge of your life and live more independently. You have realized you are not a kid anymore, and with age come responsibilities. You are entering a stage in your life where more will be expected and demanded from you. You will be held accountable for your actions. However, some youngsters tend to have trouble adapting to this new stage of their life. Some get stuck in their pre-teen years, behaving as if they are in elementary or junior high school where they can do as they please with minimal consequences. This is the stage where the problems seem to begin for some teens where they just plainly refuse to grow up or take responsibility for their actions.

They refuse to listen to their parents because they feel that they know everything. But guess what? You may know some things, but you do not know everything; you will never know everything, you will always be learning because it is a part of life.

You have reached an age where you are able to drive to school—of course, if you have a license, car and your parents' permission. Remember these are all privileges, not rights, so protect them because they can be taken away and you will lose them. Also you may now have to work, at least a part-time job, since you are at a point in your life where you need to start earning and working for the things you want. Soon you will learn that nothing in life is free. You may no longer get an allowance or the amount you are given no longer meets your needs, so working part-time is a good option for you.

In high school you may start to encounter temptations like drugs, alcohol, sex, ditching school, or you may face peer pressure by someone trying to convince you to try this or that. They will try to convince you by saying cliché phrases like: "Everyone is doing it," "Don't be a wimp" or "a coward," and "You're not cool." But no matter what you are told, the fact is that not everyone is doing it: Just say, "No thank you." Only fools fall into these traps. You are now at a point where you need to make critical and intelligent decisions. You want to fit in, be accepted by your peers, be cool and go with the flow, but you also need to be wise. Remember, you have choices and will always have choices; make sure you make wise choices.

This is where you need to think twice before deciding what you will do next, because the decisions you make today will have an impact on you for the rest of your life. When someone asks you if you want to try this new drug, or do something you know is wrong or illegal, do not even think about it. Be clear with your answer, just say no, and walk away.

Sometimes peer pressure makes you do things that normally you would not do but because you want to be liked, accepted, or want to fit in you go along with it. Oftentimes, weak young people give into peer pressure without considering the consequences; again, this could be because *everyone is doing it except you*. This is what you are told or maybe it is your "best friend" who you trust and would never lie to you, but here is the thing: Real friends would not encourage you to do things that you do not want to do, or pressure you to do things they know are wrong. And too often, we fall into the trap without considering the consequences. These so-called friends will push you to make bad decisions that will impact you for the rest of your life. These "friends" will leave you, and will move on and you will probably never see them again. But, if you listen to them, they can impact you for the rest of your life in a negative way; these friends are only using you. Remember every action has a reaction.

So before you try that first beer, smoke that first marijuana joint, take your first hookah puff, or engage in unsafe sexual activities, you need to look beyond and ask yourself: What if? What if I become addicted to alcohol or drugs? What if I get pregnant or get a disease—often incurable—, or get arrested? What if it is some other drug and I overdose? You need to consider all these things before making these bad decisions! Look beyond and picture yourself either pregnant, with a disease or hooked on drugs, or in jail, or worse, the cemetery. All because you wanted to be liked, accepted, by someone you will probably never see again in your life. Think twice before you make a decision and always do what you believe and feel in your heart are best for you and not what others think is right.

If you are still underage you may believe that things are not serious yet, and you may believe that if you get arrested nothing will happen. You may be under the impression that because you are a minor your parents can bail you out of jail the same day with a mere warning or community service, and you may even see it as funny or just a game. But once you turn eighteen you are now responsible; your parents will no longer be responsible for your actions, and they will no longer be able to bail you out. Things will become more serious, and you will have to face the music on your own. You will now be treated as an adult. You can choose to make the right decisions or wrong decisions; it is up to you whether you succeed or fail.

Many times we try to justify why we did what we did, we look for excuses to justify why we failed, why adversity made us fail, and why we were set up to fail. We may feel that we are victims of society, of the system: The system failed us, our parents failed us, our teachers failed us, or we failed because we came from a one-parent home, or we were raised by someone other than our biological parents. Sadly, these types of excuses equate taking the easy way out. We need to stop making excuses for our failures, and take responsibility for our actions.

Most of the time we are victims, but victims of our own actions. We choose to fail by making bad decisions, we choose what route to take with the choices life gives us. We can go right or wrong, we can either go through life complaining of how bad we have it and making excuses for our failures, or we can take charge of our lives now and be in control of our own destiny. Regardless of our past or present circumstances, we can either waste valuable energy making up excuses as to why we failed or we can take that energy and use it to better ourselves, to succeed in life. Often we just want to take the easy way out; we complain about how hard we have it; how we are not making it; how we are not where we want to be. But other than complain we do nothing to change our situation. We may tend to just throw our life away and then try to justify it because it is much easier to find excuses than to find solutions. We need to change that mentality, change our way of thinking by looking at things differently and more positively. If we set our mind to it we can overcome anything.

You just need to want it bad enough, work hard at it and not give up no matter what; stay encouraged and eventually all your hard work and efforts will pay off. Patience is the key. Nobody said it would be easy, and usually we want something but don't want to work for it. We may feel that we are entitled to it, that we deserve it and that it should not cost us anything, or we may feel these things are owed to us. This is called entitlement. Entitlement is when we believe that we are inherently deserving of privileges or special treatment. Some analysts have called this current generation of young people the worst, most entitled, most spoiled generation in the history of humankind. Young man, young woman, it is up to you to prove them otherwise, and to prevent them from stereotyping you with these labels.

Sometimes we focus so much of what we do not have that we forget to be thankful for what we do have. Always remember that someone else has it worse, so be thankful for what you have. Sometimes it just depends on how you feel and see things; happiness is a state of mind. Happiness should not depend on second or third-parties or on material things. You can choose to get up in the morning and say, "It's going to be a great day and nobody can ruin it for me!" Look in the mirror and repeat, "I am beautiful and I am mine, and nobody can take that away from me!" Same mentally goes for liking something you decide whether you like it or not, whether it is food, your car, your school, your friends, your neighborhood; you choose to like it or not. You choose to love or hate; too often we hear people say, "I used to like it" or "I used to love it." It is just a state of mind; you just need to change your mentality. How often do you hear people say, "I changed my mind, I do like it now," or "Now I do like that person." Sometimes you just need to clear your mind, and keep an open mind to ideas and suggestions to avoid preconceived notions of someone or something. To avoid pre-judgement and presumptions be objective, stay neutral, and gather all evidence before jumping to conclusions. Do not be fooled by appearances. In life do not assume anything before examining all the evidence. Remain impartial and always strive to make a difference in the world, make it positive, and leave your mark. Try to influence others to do the right thing. "What would God do?" This is what you need to ask yourself when not sure or confused, and always be prepared for new opportunities. Take every good opportunity presented to you because some opportunities only come once in a lifetime. Life is not always fuzzy, warm and rosy; there are ups and downs, trips and falls, wins and losses; it is all part of learning. Sometimes you need to experience defeat to savor victory and face adversity to appreciate what you have. If you accept these challenges it means you are ready to take charge of your life.

FOLLOW THE SIGNS

Plan and prioritize. It is always good to have a plan and organizing your tasks by order of importance. You need a life plan, an education plan, an employment plan, and a plan for everything. Some people go through life with plenty of plans but no action; they have plans but never place them in motion. This is just as bad as having no plans.

Life is a journey with stops and go's, turns and detours, ups and downs, different limits and signs pointing in various directions. Sometimes there are even breakdowns along the way, so before you embark on this journey you need to have a plan. You need to know your destination, to follow the signs and to be prepared for the unexpected. To plan ahead you will need a detailed map that will answer the following questions:

- Where are you going?

- How will you get there?

- When will you get there?

- What is it going to cost you?

- Who will help you?

- Why is it worth it?

- And, what's your final destination?

In life you need a plan to arrive where you need or want to go so plan your life like a long journey. Just like when driving along a highway, you need to follow the signs.

Plan ahead. Plan your education, your career, and your job. Lay it out from beginning to end, and don't leave anything to chance. Anticipate things, and stay one step ahead of adversary; poor planning results in negative results. Form a strategy and ask what comes next. Stop and look at your options, and which direction to take. Planning without action is useless so put your plan in motion. See if the boat will float, see what works, and make adjustments as you go. Prepare your game plan, strategy, and have a backup plan. Reorganize, re-group, move your players, cover all your bases, measure the outcome, the results, the score. You cannot continue doing the same things and expect different results. See what's missing. What can you do different? Step back and analyze because in life you also need a game plan, you need direction, a target, something to shoot for. Don't lose sight of your dreams or become discouraged. Don't compromise your goals or settle for less. Examine all your options. Also, do not take shortcuts; remember shortcuts often lead to dead ends. The longest route to a destination is a shortcut, so take no shortcuts with your life. Make a detailed list of what you want, what you would like your life to be, where you want to go. Make a map of how you will get there. Where do you want to live and work? What do you wish to have and what do you want to accomplish? Whatever dreams or goals, either material, spiritual, health or educational-wise, make a detailed map from start to finish and post it somewhere where you can see it. Like on your car, on a wall, or your refrigerator, make a check list to monitor your progress and keep you motivated. Make yourself accountable for your actions, focus on the goal at hand, on your budget, and do not lose focus or become distracted. Nothing else matters. Make sure to share your plans with others, since this will hold you accountable and will ensure your progress is tracked.

ALWAYS BE PREPARED AND ON GUARD

*D*o you know where you are headed? Are you ready and are you prepared?

Always be prepared for when opportunities arise. Prepare ahead of time and write out a checklist. Think ahead so you will always be prepared and on guard. You can never be too prepared for anything; expect the unexpected and train for life tasks. For example: When someone approaches you, be thinking ahead of what the person may want, what your answer may be, and your reaction. Never get defensive, just be prepared. Stay positive, but also stay vigilant. Pray for the best but prepare for any outcome.

STRATEGY

A PLAN OF ACTION

What is your strategy? A strategy is simply a plan of action you have to achieve a goal. Before engaging in any event you need to have a strategy. You need a strategy as to who, what, when, why, where, and how, in order to achieve your goals. You need to have a strategy as to when to start or slow down, pick up the pace, and when to stop. Repeat the process according to your circumstances.

All these things need to be considered when preparing your strategy. Examine the pros and cons, adjust your plan according to the conditions and situations, make necessary modifications just like a coach would during a game. Make sure you look for weak spots and change tactics. Once you have decided to engage, make your move without hesitation, and jump in with both feet. Know when to stop and examine the results, add up the score.

If you feel you are still not prepared, do not make a move. Do not attempt it until you feel you are ready; the higher the climb the harder the fall, so be prepared. What may work for others may not work for you, or what worked yesterday may not necessarily work today. Keep in mind, if there is nothing to be gained from what you are doing, then do not move forward with your strategy. Pick your battles carefully, under your terms, when you feel you have the advantage and odds are on your side, go for it.

When you are strategizing, figure out what the best route is and why, change routes when necessary, and have a backup plan. Always know who you are dealing with, what their record is, their strategy, and if they play by the rules. Never get too overconfident or let victories go to your head.

ONLY YOU CAN MAKE IT A REALITY

A famous American writer said this partial quote, "Action speaks louder than words," and it could not be any truer. As a young adult you need to take full responsibility for your actions, since you will be held accountable for them. Make sure your actions reflect your words and thoughts, so they do not impact you in a negative way. Know when to take action, and let your actions be positive and productive.

Always be prepared to take action, but first weigh your options before moving forward and engaging. Always try to reason with people, listen to their side of the story, their point of view, even if you don't agree. Remember, to succeed in life you need to take action. To catch dreams you first need to chase them. Nothing comes from dreaming if not followed by action. Also, you need to watch negative actions because the day will come when we will regret them; you will feel sorry but it might be too late to change things. Stop and think before you act, visualize the outcome, and look farther than your goal.

Keep in mind that the only person that can make things possible is you; only you can create it, only you can visualize it, and only you can make it a reality. Only you can make it happen.

QUALITY

TAKE SOMETHING AND MAKE IT BETTER

*A*lways concentrate on producing quality work; your job depends on it. Measure quality, always look for ways to improve and take pride in your work. Even when you think you are doing a great job, there is always room for continuous improvement. Whether in your personal life, school or at home, are you living a quality life? If you did well today, you can do better tomorrow. Think of ways on how you can improve and make it better. Stick to it until it's perfected by paying attention to detail.

What qualities do you have and are you exploiting all of them? Are you doing things right the first time? If you don't have time to do it correctly the first time, how will you find time to do it a second or third time? Quality needs to be high on your list of standards, and you should never settle for mediocrity or anything less than one hundred percent quality. Make your good better and develop your better to best! Take something and make it perfect.

DO NOT WASTE VALUABLE TIME

*D*edicate yourself one hundred percent to your cause, your mission or to whatever it may be that you are working on or involved in. Choose your cause wisely and finish what you start whether it's school, work, family matters or sports. Stay committed because hard work and dedication equal success. Focus on things that matter by looking at the big picture and not worrying about little insignificant things or issues that are not helping your cause. Always ask yourself: What did I accomplish today? And, what do I want to accomplish tomorrow? Dedicate yourself to perfecting your trade.

Always strive to have feelings of success and acceptance, and be persistent in maintaining a positive outlook. Perseverance, hard work and dedication will lead you to accomplish your goals. This often means sacrificing all other useless activities for the sake of your goals and dreams, and this is done by focusing all your energy and your resources on achieving them. Do not settle for less! Focus on your target goal, and do not worry about what others are or are not doing or saying. Concentrate on your stuff and do not compare yourself to others; the only one you need to compare yourself with is the "yesterday you" to the "you today." You will see results if you are dedicated completely. Do not stop halfway and wonder if you could have; you will never know unless you try. Do not waste valuable time, energy and resources fighting other people's battles, particularly those you cannot win, or battles where you have nothing to gain. Dedicate yourself to your cause only, make a list of what you want, and what you want to accomplish in life.

RUN WITH YOUR GOALS

*U*se your valuable energy on positive things that matter the most and are on your agenda. It is important to channel your energy on your plans, on positive things like your education, your family, your health, your job and your future. Focus on things that matter, encouraging and positive activities, constructive energy and good vibes. Surround yourself with enthusiastic people, those who replenish your positive energy, help you advance and encourage you by cheering you on. Keep in mind that regardless of what you do, some people will still be critical of you, even if you say yes or no, or black or white. You will find that a high percentage of people will criticize you or not agree with your decision, so stick to your plan, stick to your purpose. Run with your goals, and whatever you do, make sure you do it with faith and love.

Stress and anxiety are sometimes good companions and indicators that you are committed to your cause, because they force us to act.

They push us into action; these emotions force us to make our move, to act, to do it, to go for it, instead of sitting around in our comfort zone. If you are stressed or anxious this could be a good sign. This is all just energy ready to work, indicators that you are still focused on your goals, something that shows you are serious about success, that you are committed and are not complacent. Once you have reached your goals the stress and anxiety will go away, and you can begin to enjoy your accomplishments. And after you reach a milestone, focus on your next task, goal or assignment.

EFFORT
GIVE YOUR BEST DAY IN AND DAY OUT

Always put forth your best effort. When you give one hundred percent you compete, but when you endeavor one hundred ten percent you succeed. Everyone says they give one hundred percent, but to reach the top, to succeed and triumph, it takes more than that. You must give a little extra, a little more sacrifice, a little more sweat, a little more pain, a few more tears, a few more scratches, a few more blisters. You need the extra ten percent that will carry you to the top. Never be afraid to give a little more than is asked or expected of you. Go the extra mile, go a little longer, a little higher, dig a little deeper, a little more effort; be in it to win it. If you come just to play you might as well just stay home. You have to be willing to go above and beyond the call of duty, be proud of what you do, and do it to the best of your abilities. Give your best, day in and day out. Remember success has no days off so be consistent, give more of yourself and push yourself down to your last drop of energy.

WAIT FOR THE RIGHT TIMING

*A*n advantage is defined as the condition or circumstance that puts us in a favorable or superior position. Look for the advantage, the edge, seek your God-given talents for those things that you excel in. Look for gaps that others aren't filling, or take a different approach, a different route, or use a different strategy. Always use everything to your advantage and stay current on trends, technics, new technology and methods. Track what they are doing different, wait for the right timing to make your move, and do not engage until you feel you are ready and everything is in place. Ensure all your bases are covered. However, never take advantage of the weak, the helpless, the sick, the poor or those down on their luck.

MAKE THE MOST OF WHAT YOU HAVE

*A*s a young person who is becoming a young adult, chances are you are getting ready to obtain a job or are already working. As you begin to earn an income, you are likely to begin spending money on things you need and want. Your possessions eventually may turn into resources that you can use to achieve what you want in life. Or they can make you their slave...

Be resourceful with what God gives you: your skills and talents, your time and money. Find ways to get by with what you have, make it work. Be prepared to sustain yourself through hard times, and save for rainy days. Conserve and share your resources, and use them wisely. The fact is we live in a very materialistic world, in societies that have placed money above the most fundamental life values. Do not be a slave to material things. Ask yourself: Do I really need this, or am I just trying to fill a void that only God can fill? To be completely free in your life you need to get rid of superfluous material things, those things that you do not need, that do not bring you happiness or peace. As the saying goes: Money can buy you a bed but not sleep. Oftentimes, material things only bring more headaches and stress, and make you a slave to your possessions. Use the resources that God has given you, make the most of them, develop all your talents, use them to better yourself and to help others, and find ways to improvise and make it work. Be resourceful with your talents. Do not live beyond your means or on credit.

The world is full of examples of very wealthy people who sooner or later end up broke. Manage your resources well; no matter how much money you make, it will never be enough unless you manage it well. Learn to administer your finances properly; the key is to eliminate what you do not need, or things that are not part of your plan, goals, or that will not contribute to your planned end result. Do not buy on impulse, give yourself time to think it over; chances are you do not really need it. Learn to stretch your resources; learn to live with what you have at the moment. Make the best of it. Sometimes we need to sacrifice one thing to achieve another; save now, sacrifice temporary pleasures today, for the big goal tomorrow. Make the most of what you have.

BE VIGILANT

*I*n life you need to be cautious by watching everything you do and looking out for number one. Caution is the care we take to avoid danger or mistakes. Kind of like when you are driving your car: You follow the traffic and street signs; when you come up to an intersection you look to the left, right, in front and behind and then proceed with caution. The same applies to your life, so be very vigilant. Look at the pros and cons, prepare your moves carefully, always think of the potential consequences, and picture the end result. Approach people with caution, and when others approach you use caution, never letting your guard down. Never turn your back on traffic or on those you don't trust. Follow directions, safety guidelines, and do not take shortcuts when it comes to your safety. Be vigilant with strangers or someone you don't trust. As with everything in life you need to follow the signs, stay out of rumors and gossip, or hearsay. Do not allow yourself to be pushed or fooled into doing something you are not comfortable with or sure about.

Sometimes you have to be distrusting, so at those times trust no one but yourself. Be aware of your surroundings, anticipate things, and never assume anything. Know your limits, and do not exceed them. Avoid temptation of false riches or promises of fast get-rich schemes. There are no instant success shortcuts. *Fast don't last, but slow will flow.*

NEVER BELIEVE LAWS DO NOT APPLY TO YOU

*R*espect the law; although you sometimes may not agree with it, you need to obey the law. We need laws to preserve order. Laws are enacted for a reason, to keep order and protect you. Never believe laws do not apply to you, so follow the rules, support and help protect the laws. Avoid civil disobedience because the last thing you need is a criminal record. Oftentimes, you may be tempted to break the law to show off, to impress your friends and too look cool, but always consider the consequences, and have a set of rules to live by. When police pull you over do not become defensive or rude; wait for the officer to come to you, stay in your car, unless instructed to get out of the vehicle, and allow the officer to explain why you were pulled over. Be nice, be polite, and apologize to the officer if you missed the stop sign or the speed limit or whatever it may be. If you are polite, most likely you will get a break. But don't speak until the officer asks you to, and do not raise your voice, stay calm.

TACKLE ISSUES HEAD ON

Problems are part of our lives. Some may be good problems and other bad problems. Good problems help us overcome obstacles to achieve our goals. Positive problems are opportunities to grow and make our lives better and more prosperous. Negative problems, on the other hand, are those we create for ourselves, usually for behaving irresponsibly or negligently. In any case, we need to face our problems, whether they are positive or negative.

But let's face it: The best way to get out of a problem is to avoid getting into one in the first place. If you look for problems you are going to find them, guaranteed. Before you make any important decisions, it is always best to allow enough time to think about it. If you have gotten yourself into a bad situation, you need to have a different mind-set than that which you had at the beginning.

Try to avoid problems and problematic people altogether. Some individuals always seem to be getting into trouble; you need to stay away from them before they get you wrapped up in their mess, their problems, or their drama. Don't be an involuntary accomplice. Stay clear of those who like to draw others into their messy, sticky web; they only want to draw attention to themselves in a negative way, always looking for trouble, always miserable, and they seem to enjoy bringing their misery and suffering to other people. Seek and you shall find, so if you seek peace, you will find peace. If you seek trouble you will find it; trouble follows no one, this is a myth; troublemakers follow, find and make trouble. If you bring a problem upon yourself do not try to justify your actions by making yourself look like a victim; you are only a victim of your own actions.

Often, we hear some individuals after they get in trouble say: "It was meant to happen." Well this is another myth; it happened because he or she caused it. Just like vehicle accidents do not just happen, they are caused by distracted drivers.

Yelling, screaming, or making a scene will get you nowhere; there are other options to help you solve your problems with positive outcomes. Issues need to be tackled head on, so do not avoid or ignore them. Resolve them, since ignoring a problem will not make it go away and disappear like magic. By ignoring it, you are allowing the problem to grow out of control. It is much easier to put out a small fire than a giant inferno. Do not allow things to escalate.

TEMPTATION COMES IN ALL SHAPES, SIZES AND FORMS

A temptation is a desire to do something, especially something wrong or unwise. Usually, temptation leads us to trouble, so we need to be constantly watching what we desire. As a young person you need to avoid being tempted by any kind of false promises, such as promises of easy money. What costs nothing is worth nothing. Easy money comes with side effects.

Temptation comes in all shapes, sizes and forms so do not be fooled with false promises of an easy life, drugs, money, love, and fancy things. Do not fall for get rich schemes; there is no such thing as overnight success. You need to work for real success, everything else is just a fantasy, fool's gold. Get-rich-quick schemes are a quick ticket to jail, or worse, the cemetery. Do not fall prey to these types of ruses. When someone asks you if you want to make a quick easy buck, just say, "No thank you. I like to work hard for my money. I like to earn my things and what I make."

WRONG CROWDS

KNOW THE PEOPLE YOU HANG OUT WITH

When people get in trouble, their main excuse is that they got caught up with the wrong crowd. Reality check: You chose to hang out with the wrong crowd. You decided to join them and be part of their group. Do not get caught up with the wrong crowd, gang, hate group, or with negative people who have their own personal agenda. They will promise you a place, a family, security and protection in order to create a false sense of belonging. They will suck you in with false promises to promote their cause and use you for their purpose. Associating yourself with these groups will result in terrible consequences; these people are not your family. Their so-called code of silence only exists in movies because in real life these people will turn against you in a second to save their own skin. When arrested or confronted they will talk and say anything to save themselves, and at the first chance they will abandon you. Your family is the only real family you have; they will always be there through thick and thin, your ups and downs, good times and bad times. Others will only use you for their purpose. They may promise protection, but ask yourself, "Protection from whom or what, from gangs?" If you don't become involved with gangs, you will not need protection. It is always best to remain neutral. Do not be pressured into joining a group who has their own agenda. When they ask you to join just say, "No thanks." You cannot soar like an eagle when you're hanging out with turkeys. Know the people you hang out with, and make a conscious choice to be friends with folks who will influence your life in a positive manner. In other words: Hang out with the right crowd.

CONFLICTS

AVOID DIFFICULT PEOPLE

Never make life more complicated than it already is. Simply avoid conflicts at all cost. There will always be difficult people, and individuals that are hard to deal with, who have personal issues, or those who are looking for a fight with the first person they encounter. Some people are not looking for a solution; they are only looking for trouble. Please do not fall into their trap, and do not play along with their games. Sadly, these individuals carry a great deal of trash in their lives and are looking for a place to dispose of it; do not be their dumpster. Young man, young woman, you will always encounter difficult people with negative attitudes towards everything. It is wiser to turn and walk away than try to reason or deal with these individuals. Do not try to be brave; you have nothing to prove and nothing to gain and you do not need to fight to prove you are correct.

Oftentimes, you may believe the problem is with you, but it is not, so do not tempt, do not push, do not dare these people into action which you may later regret. Never argue just for the sake of arguing. Arguing with ignorant people will get you nowhere; it will only bring you stress. Arguing with these people is like wrestling in the mud with pigs; after a few rounds you finally realize the pigs love it. Some people wake up and their only intention is to ruin someone else's day, do not fall victim, avoid these folks at all costs, they are easy to identify.

BE A GOOD EXAMPLE TO OTHERS

*D*o you feel pressure to behave in a certain way because your friends or people in your group expect it? If so, you have experienced peer pressure. When faced with peer pressure, be smart and cautious. Stay safe and out of trouble by plainly passing up risky opportunities your friends and peers may want you to become involved with. When friends ask you to drink, smoke hookah or do drugs, just walk away and let them know you don't do that stuff. It's that simple. Whatever their response is, don't let it bother you. You have to be above that, have your own mind; you are more than capable of deciding what is best for your life and future. When you allow others to pressure you into doing things you do not agree with, then you have just handed them control of your destiny. You may believe everyone is doing it, but you are simply with a crowd that is engaging in bad behavior or illegal activities, and once you get away from these types of people, you will find that not everyone is doing it. Whether it is drugs, alcohol, violence, or sexual promiscuity, peer pressure comes in many shapes and forms. Embed this in your mind; it only takes one time. One time to overdose, one time to die from alcohol poisoning, one time to become a daddy or mommy, and just one time to end up in prison.

On the other hand, do not pressure or influence others into participating in bad behavior. Do not tease them or dare them. Violence is not cool, bullying or hurting others is not cool, no matter what they tell you. Do not encourage others to be violent, don't be part of it, do not be an accomplice, and always remember if you are not part of the solution then you are part of the problem. Be a good example to others. Be the antidote to peer pressure.

A bully is a person who threatens to hurt someone, often forcing that person to do something. Bullying is wrong, it's against the law, it hurts people, and can land those who engage in it in legal trouble.

No one likes a bully! All bullies are just a bunch of cowards! They are individuals who feel inferior and worthless, and therefore, picking on other people makes them feel superior or better about themselves and gives them a sense of satisfaction.

Being cruel to others who are weaker or defenseless is wrong no matter how you slice it; bullying is wrong! Bullies are predators who look for easy prey, and victims that will not fight back. They like to frighten, threaten, and insult their victims for no apparent reason other than to try and feel superior. Bullies may believe that harassing or hurting other people physically or mentally is funny. But it is not funny, it is wrong and illegal. Before picking on others and bullying them, put yourself in their shoes so you can experience what they feel. It may not always be physical but mental aggression, like ignoring others, avoiding them, excluding them, or making fun of them. Or for no apparent reason making them cry or feel miserable. As people increasingly engage in online activities, the term *cyberbullying* has become a trend, leading some victims to commit suicide after *cyberbullies* have made them their target of mean-spirited social media attacks and fake social media accounts.

It is everyone's responsibility to prevent it from happening and we all need to do our part. If you see bullying you need to speak up, get involved, tell someone, report it by telling your parents, school personnel, friends, your pastor, or the police. Do not be afraid to speak up. If you are being bullied report it immediately. Do not be intimidated and know that you are not the problem. Bullies are the problem; they may just be jealous of you, because you are a better person than them.

TAKE YOUR LIFE SERIOUS

*L*ife is full of risks so never take unnecessary ones. Be aware of individuals who just want to provoke fights for no apparent reason. Do not try to be a hero or the one who always saves the day. You do not always have to be the Good Samaritan; sometimes it is best to not get involved in other people's business unless you are protecting yourself or a loved one, or there is something to be gained, or to save something or someone. Do not risk it, always weigh your options and don't endanger your health, life, freedom, or your relationships. Follow your instincts, and ask yourself what is at risk. There will always be someone better, stronger, and bigger than you. We live in a sometimes cruel world, so the key is survival, so be smart.

When you're walking or driving to school and someone calls you names or calls you out, be smart and just keep going. Ignore them. Be wise, and don't become trapped in their snares. You are smarter than they are; do not allow yourself to be trapped. Keep your distance, say nothing and continue on your way. Never become overly aggressive, and always stay in control of the situation.

If you find yourself in a situation where law enforcement detains you, let them do their job, listen to them first, and do not get an attitude because if you make their job difficult they will make your life miserable. They can make it easy or you can make it hard. They are getting paid so they can take as long as they want and give you all the citations for the laws they believe you violated. It's always best to receive your citation and move on. Oftentimes, if you are nice, cooperative and behave courteously, you may get a break.

Never push individuals to their limits, by teasing, daring or tempting them. The only risks we should sometimes take are with business decisions, but not with your life.

Don't wait to hit bottom to make changes in your life. Avoid the road to destruction by not being fooled or pressured by friends because after they are gone, you will be the only one left to face the music alone. You will be the one holding the ball, so do not be fooled by others. Some people have issues and become offended just by someone looking at them. Be careful with individuals who have mental health issues, and others who are just not well. You do not know how some people perceive things. Although we may be looking at the same object we may all see, hear and feel something different. We all tend to only see what we want to see.

Never rush into a situation. Remember that drugs and alcohol destroy lives and that it is much easier not to get into a situation than it is to get out of it. Never trust anyone but yourself, never let your guard down, and never think that you are bulletproof. You only have one life, so you need to take good care of it because once you lose it, you will not get it back; do not risk it. Life is very precious, take care of yours by never putting it at risk just to please your friends or to show off because once you are gone, no one is going to care. The only ones you need to please are you, your parents and God.

Do not get involved in dangerous or foolish activities or risky pranks. Always think of the consequences, the end result. Careless activities and horseplay usually have terrible consequences. Imagine if you break or lose a limb, become paralyzed, brain-damaged, disfigured or lose your eyesight. Or worst, if you cause someone else to get hurt, you will be liable. So look at all the risks involved in careless activities or pranks.

Some people have a very short fuse or personal issues, others are just mentally and emotionally unstable individuals, and consequently it is best not to become involved with these types of people. They have their own agenda. On the other hand, you have your own plans, and should not include them. Remember that life is already full of dangers and hazards, therefore, don't create anymore by being reckless or careless. Don't lose control of even one second because that action within that second can result in a life of regret. It only takes a moment to lose control. Always think of the consequences.

Government statistics show that one out of every four youngsters will be charged with a crime by the time they are twenty-four years old. The ages between eighteen and twenty-one is when you are at the greatest risk, the most vulnerable age. Once a teenager turns eighteen he or she will be charged as an adult, and maybe even before depending on the crime. This is because at eighteen, a young person is considered an adult by law. This is also the age when young people begin to have more freedom, sometimes more than they can handle, or more than they know what to do with. At this age youngsters start to feel more daring and invincible. They want to consume the world, they feel like they always have something to prove, and they end up putting themselves in harm's way. They feel they have much courage, but some of them become a statistic.

Remember, courage means facing your fears, and stupidity is to fear nothing. Always watch what you do, analyze your actions, think of how you are hurting yourself by those actions and don't even know the irreversible damage you may be causing yourself or others. Don't ruin your life or the life of others by your careless acts, only to please your friends or to show off.

Never take what is not yours, whether it is material things or credit for something you did not do. Always make wise and intelligent choices by being well-informed. Weigh the pros and cons, life is not a game, and you are playing for keeps. Any negative action can have dire consequences. You need to learn to control aggressive impulses, do not act on them. Practice positive, social, constructive and helpful behavior. You need to take your life serious, your education, your career, your health, and your family.

PROMOTE LOVE AND LIFE

*A*s a young person you need to realize that love is the only and true way to have a fulfilling life. Don't harbor hate, it destroys you from within. Avoid haters and do not hang around with people that hate. Do not be others' dumpster for their hateful waste. Allow love to build your life and lead your path. Do not let hate destroy your life and your soul. Avoid causing harm to others, either physically or mentally. Do not promote hate. Don't tolerate it! Learn to forgive and move on. Avoid getting involved with hate groups. Instead, promote love and life, and join groups that foster these fundamental human values. After all, hate is no match for love.

CONFRONTATIONS

LEARN TO DEFUSE A SITUATION

*A*re you a confrontational young person? If you tend to deal with situations in an aggressive way, or you are hostile or argumentative, then chances are this characteristic will lead you to confrontations. Avoid confrontations at all costs, especially when they start to get out of hand. Just state your business and move on, do not waste precious energy on unnecessary confrontations where there is nothing to be gained. It is best to just turn and walk away. Do not fall into traps. Do not risk your life or your health. There are some people who you cannot reason with, some people have personal issues or are sick and seem to always be looking for a fight. Learn to defuse a situation, to calm your nerves, and calm the crowd. Do not allow confrontations to become violent. When you go into a meeting keep in mind you are there to find a solution, not to confront, not to point fingers, or to find fault or humiliate. Remember, any confrontation should result with a positive outcome.

STAY IN CONTROL

Anger is one of the strongest feelings of annoyance, displeasure, or hostility that we human beings experience. Anger can get you into trouble. Avoid getting angry as much as you can because it will get you nowhere. Keep a cool head, breathe deep, think positive, calm your nerves, and do not lose control. Cooler heads always prevail and think clearer. If you feel you are about to lose it, excuse yourself, just get up and go for a walk or a drive.

When it comes to making important decisions, never make them while you are angry, since anger does not help you think clearly. The steam from your hot temper won't allow you to make the right decisions and you may say things that are hurtful and that you do not really mean, which you will regret later. Angry people tend to offend, and this can have grave consequences if you offend the wrong person. If you get angry, never let it be obvious; always strive to stay in control. It is said that when people manage to make you angry, they have won the battle. Always state your business, leave quietly, and nobody gets hurt. The key about anger here is to control it. Anger can also make you feel resentment towards others, and this will get you nowhere. Insulting or taking your frustration out on others is wrong. If someone did you wrong you need to be able to forgive and move on. Some individuals have a difficult time forgiving because of pride or ego, but you need to leave all behind and forgive. Carrying anger inside of you is very unhealthy and it will end by eating you up. If God forgives our sins, then why do we find it so hard to forgive others?

Avoid having an angry attitude or going into rages. Sometimes you will just need to release some of that tension, so before you break; relax and breathe deep, go for a walk or run and allow yourself time to cool down. If you encounter someone who is angry, never try to match their anger with yours. Remember the mirror effect: Do not imitate what the other person is doing, learn to diffuse the situation, stay in control and do not lose it. If you cannot reason with these individuals, just walk away.

Work with your character and learn how to deal with your emotions. Identify things that make you angry and anticipate them so you can maintain control. Know how to respond to anger and to turn it around to maintain happiness in your life. Seek out help if you feel you cannot control your anger. Talk to a counselor or teacher at school, a pastor, your mom or dad, anyone who you feel can help you.

AGGRESSION AND RETALIATION

PROMOTE PEACE AND HARMONY

Our first natural reaction when someone hurts or offends us is to hurt them back, but this is wrong. If someone did you wrong, don't retaliate or seek revenge.

Avoid aggression and violence at all costs. A hostile environment is very unhealthy. When we become frustrated, sometimes our first reaction is aggression, whether it is to injure or destroy, cause pain or damage, but you need to stay away from promoting, provoking or instigating aggression. Aggression usually leads to more aggression; an eye for an eye will result in a blind world. Violence only leads to more violence; therefore, promote peace and harmony. We have choices, so we can choose to be part of the problem or part of the solution.

Aggressive or violent individuals just see a person as just another victim or prey to lash out at, but somebody loves them. They could be someone's father, grandfather, son, daughter, sister, or brother, so always keep this in mind before you act since you can hurt third parties.

Think before you become aggressive or violent or cause harm to others. It takes two, so don't be a victim to someone else's aggression; don't be the secondary party. Never take your anger out on innocent people. When someone yells, do not yell back. If they insult you, do not insult back. If they assault you, do not assault back. Do not shadow because two wrongs do not make a right. Learn to forgive and forget, leave the rest to God. Pray for them so they may find peace. To be able to stay in control and not lose it, is not a sign of weakness but one of strength.

Finally, remember that you can denounce aggression through legitimate channels, and that the legal system is in place precisely so we do not live under the "an eye for an eye" practice, known as the law of retaliation. Our laws hold the principle that if an individual has injured another individual, the perpetrator is to be penalized to a similar degree, and the victim is to receive an estimated value of that injury in a fair compensation.

DON'T TRY TO IMPRESS OTHERS

*B*efore you start questioning everything bad that is happening in your life, do a self-evaluation first. You may just be a victim of your own attitude, actions and thoughts. You may think you are bad and that nobody can touch you. That nobody is better than you, that you are invincible and tough. You may believe nobody can mess with you, that everyone fears you, and that you have a reputation of being bad; but guess what? There will always be someone "badder" than you. Prisons and cemeteries are full of individuals who also thought they were brave and bad. Don't try to impress others or show off by acting bad. Don't make a fool out of yourself trying to draw attention by doing foolish things that you will later regret. No matter how bad you think you are, there will always be someone "badder," meaner and stronger. The people or the friends you try to impress by being bad won't even remember you once you are in prison; you will be the one living with the consequences.

Instead of being bad, try to be a good example to others. Be a leader especially to those younger than you. Impress them with good grades, by being obedient to your parents, respectful to your teachers, and by living a life that is pleasing to God.

TRUTHFULNESS

ALWAYS TELL THE TRUTH

*B*e truthful to yourself, to your cause, to your teammates, your friends, and to your family. Be sincere with all of your relations, when you say you are going to do something, do it, and do it like you mean it, stick to the facts, and don't make stuff up. Always tell the truth. Tell it like it is. Get to the point. The truth will set you free. Remember that half-truths are also lies in disguise. Lying is equal to cheating, and cheating equals to lying. Lying is a monster that eventually will catch up with you. When you lie you lose credibility and even when you say the truth, lying puts your character into question. When you say something no one will believe you because you will be labeled as a liar, and liars are the only ones that believe their lies; they say a lie to cover another lie. Always speak with the truth, no matter what.

THINK BEFORE YOU SPEAK

Communication is very important. Always communicate your intentions, don't assume anything, ensure everyone is on the same page and that they understand your message, and then ask for feedback. Avoid unnecessary misunderstandings and confusion caused by poor communication. When you give or receive instructions repeat them back. Keep an open mind, and gather all the information before making a decision or jumping to conclusions.

Good communicators can obtain anything in life. As a young person, you need to work hard to develop your communication skills, since they will be one of your best assets. Practice communication, become articulate, and have fluency when you speak. Think before you speak, repeat in your mind what you are going to say before opening your mouth, rehearse it. Listening is an important part of communication, so practice active listening. You need to echo, resonate, clarify, and know what you are talking about. If you do not understand what you are saying no one else will, and when you speak, be convincing.

Always think before you speak, keep conversations interesting, and keep in mind that sometimes humor helps break the ice. Do not offend or hurt someone with your words. Once words leave your mouth you cannot bring them back, so speak clearly, state your business, make your point and stop. If you speak too much you'll lose credibility. No one listens to those who speak too much. Always be open to suggestions, listen to other points of view, and wait for your turn to speak.

Don't give your opinion unless asked, and choose your words wisely by knowing your audience and your topic. Stick to your subject, get to the point and don't get sidetracked. When you speak use some body language like your hands and facial expressions to go along with your speech to help drive your message home. Practice in front of the mirror your communication skills.

When necessary, do not be afraid to speak up for others who can't speak for themselves, or fend for themselves. Speak up for those who do not have a voice, for the persecuted, the sick, and the unwanted.

THANK GOD FOR TEACHERS

Besides our parents, good teachers and coaches should be the only role models we look up to since it is their career to educate, train, and equip us. Teachers deserve more credit than they receive. Respect them, support them, listen to them, and value them since they are the key to your success. Everything we learn in our school career we learn from teachers, from writing our first letter to reading our first word, to writing our first essay. So thank you teachers and thank God for teachers.

Teachers are one of your best resources for success, the ones who can help you succeed in life and help you thrive. They play a critical role in your life; they help prepare you for life, your future and for success. Great and dedicated teachers should be your only true role models, mentors, and true heroes. We need to honor our teachers. They are America's true heroes, including coaches who teach us discipline, respect, hard work, dedication, responsibility, and teamwork.

Teachers are often mentors but there are other people who can mentor you in a particular way. Look in your community for someone to mentor you, and then spend a good deal of your time being mentored. A person who can serve as mentors could be someone who is already doing what you want to do in life, someone more experienced, knowledgeable, older and wiser. All successful people have had at least one mentor.

READING IS KNOWLEDGE

The average person only reads one book per year, but if you were to read two books a month, in five years you could be an expert on almost any subject. Make good use of your spare time by reading, fill your mind with knowledge. Buy your own books or go to your school or local public library to check out books, e-books or audio books. If you drive a vehicle to school or work, you can listen to audio books in your car. The average person drives 12,000 miles a year, so if you were to listen to audio books instead of popular music while driving, in three years you could have a knowledge comparable to that obtained in a two-year college education. Choose your books wisely, in whatever platform you prefer, but attain the knowledge found in reading or listening to audio books. Invest time in reading and you will become knowledgeable in many areas and possibly an expert in your area of interest.

CONSUMING THE DARKNESS OF IGNORANCE

Your education is very important, and yes you can accomplish it! Most of us have the same aptitude, we are all capable of learning, and it's a choice we make. Intelligence is having the mental capacity to learn from experiences, solve problems, and use this acquired knowledge to adapt to new situations. Education is the light that consumes the darkness of ignorance, the answer to freedom, peace, and justice.

To change your life, and the world, you need an education. Learning does not consist of only repeating what others are saying, or what others are doing or have done in the past: Education is more about trying new things and new ideas. Wisdom comes from experience and experience comes from mistakes, and for education to begin you need to question everything you see, hear, feel or read. This will result in true knowledge. Life is full of experiments, so you need to find what works and does not work. This experience will lead to knowledge, and then to wisdom. Place value on your education and not so much value on material things like jewelry and cars; the only thing that should matter to you is your education.

Oftentimes, you can get carried away or get caught up in the garbage you see or hear through music and media outlets. Much of what you hear nowadays glorifies cars, jewelry, sneakers, drugs, fast money, easy hook-ups, violence and crime. You should only value your education, your family, your health; invest now on important things for your life that will pay dividends in the future.

As a young person, your education should come first. It's sad to see young individuals throw their education away for temporary pleasures or luxuries, or for things that have no value for that matter. Education is not only about learning how to make a living but how to live. Education is forever, so it can never be taken away from you. It can sometimes be expensive but ignorance is more expensive. Invest in your education now. It will pay interest later in life, guaranteed. Education starts and continues at home; we learn through teaching, and learn by teaching others. Some say education is hard, but remember if the road was so easy it's probably not worth the trip.

Education is the only weapon you need in life. It's the most powerful weapon to combat ignorance. Educate and exercise your mind. Education, intelligence and ignorance are all choices. We are all ignorant when we are born and many stay that way by choice. With all the information at our fingertips there is no excuse for not obtaining an education. Without education you are like a bird without wings, flightless. To rule the world you need an education because it is knowledge, and knowledge is power when it is put to use, power is respect, and respect is peace and happiness.

Education starts when you question something; knowledge starts when you find the answers to your questions. Knowledge is something you keep, they can take everything away from you except your knowledge. Teach others what you know. When we teach we also learn in the process, we need to share our knowledge, our experience, save others from making the same mistakes we've made. Remember what you learn today will aid in your success tomorrow. The more you learn the more you can earn, so expand your knowledge and learn as much as possible in all subjects like science, math, technology, politics, finance, health and so on. All subjects are interrelated. Learn about current trends as well, all this information will be helpful in holding conversations with anyone.

Learn a new language; people who speak more than one language have a great advantage. Yes, speaking a second language has many benefits in this global economy. Employers see a benefit in hiring multilingual so you will have greater employment opportunities. Society is now multi-racial, learning a second language allows you to interact with all kinds of people with different backgrounds and cultures. You will be able to engage with more people by speaking a second or third language.

As you embark in getting an education, it is important that you think about the following statistics; the negatives of dropping out of high school are quite clear:

- Every 26 seconds a student drops out of high school (according to the report *The Silent Epidemic: Perspectives of High School Dropouts*).

- Students who don't graduate from high school are more likely to end up in prison, more likely to live in poverty, more likely to suffer from health issues (U.S. Department of Education).

- Students who don't graduate from high school have a higher unemployment rate (72% more likely to be unemployed, U.S. Department of Labor).

- Students who don't graduate high school earn a lot less than those who graduate (64% less according to After School Alliance).

- According to U.S. Department of Health Services, high school dropouts are eight times more likely to end up in prison.

- According to the Office of Juvenile Justice and Delinquency Prevention, 80% of prisoners do not have a high school diploma.

- A one-year increase in average education levels would reduce arrest rates by 11% (Alliance for Excellent Education).

So if you think you don't need an education, think again. Keep in mind we can fake anything but intelligence or ignorance is very hard to conceal.

STAY ON TOP OF THINGS

*B*e proactive instead of reactive, rather than spending your life solving problems, prevent them. Make yourself useful at all times, don't wait for that phone call, you make the call before they call you. Be in control of the situation, stay in charge, and one step ahead. Being proactive means you forecast and anticipate things before they happen and you take action before others do. Therefore, when a difficult situation arises you are prepared. Do not wait for things to happen, make them happen, stop waiting and get the ball rolling.

Plan ahead, nobody ever says I am going to grow up to be a failure; it happens because they failed to plan. People do not plan to fail, they fail to plan. Do not mistake actions for achievements, just working and looking busy is not the same as being proactive. Always do things with urgency, handle situations as they arise, pay your bills on time before they are due, do not wait until the last minute, and pay your debts on time. Credit determines your character, take care of it.

You need to take care of tasks as they present themselves, take care of problems before they arise, do it today because tomorrow new ones may arise. Do not let things stockpile. Proactiveness is key; stay on top of things, do them under your terms rather than waiting then rushing to do them and finish a task last minute and trying to improvise. Plan ahead and cover all bases, remember if anything can go wrong it probably will, so pray for the best, and prepare for the worst.

As my dad would say, "Always make yourself useful and you will always be welcomed, you will always fit in, you will be okay, there will always be a place for you." Whether it is at home, work, school, church or sports, always do your best no matter what it is. Remember that poor performance or poor effort equals to poor results; always give your best no matter what, no excuses.

LEADERSHIP

MAKE A DIFFERENCE

*L*eaders provide direction and inspiration to accomplish common goals. Although you are a young person, you can develop leadership skills and begin preparing to lead. Do not be afraid to lead, to make decisive decisions, and make bold moves. Get others to follow, be an example for them, take charge and stand up for others. Learn to be a confident leader in your decisions even though you may not always make the correct decision or the most popular one, a leader's job is to make the best one. In order for you to lead, you need to gain the trust of others because if they trust you and your decisions, they will follow. If they believe in you they will trust you. Dare to be different, unique, do not try and please the crowd, design your fashion, and invent your own style.

Always try to set a trend, to make a difference in the world. Remember, in a team every member's actions affect the rest of the team. When you fail, the whole team fails. Each one of your members is an important link, and when one breaks the whole chain breaks and all falls apart.

Leaders lead by example, hard work and dedication. Don't try to make others do something you would not do yourself. Do not be afraid of getting your hands dirty and in the trenches with the team. Vision is what makes leaders. Leaders look for solutions and they see opportunities where others see obstacles. Followers look for faults rather than solutions, while leaders make paths where there is no path, and leave a trail for others to follow. Leaders obtain results, inspire others to follow, but a leader is only as good as the team he leads, so leaders need to create strong followers. As a leader others rely on you to lead them in the right direction, to lead them into victory, triumph and success. As a leader others look up to you, so watch your movements, watch what you do to support that image.

Look for opportunities to begin practicing leadership skills, get connected with community and student groups, and be ready to lead when the moment arrives.

DO NOT BE AFRAID OF CHANGE

Whether we like it or not, change is going to happen in our lives. Take a look, young man and woman, during the last few years you have dramatically changed from being a child and teenager to the person you now see in the mirror. Not only has your physical appearance changed, but the way you think and perceive things have changed as well, and they will continue to change as you mature. You may love and like some of these changes, and dislike and resist others, but change won't stop from happening.

Embrace change; do not fear what is new and different, adapt to change and your changing environment. Anything that stands still dies or is forgotten, it becomes extinct. You must be able to adapt to change if you are to survive, so support change.

Dinosaurs are no longer around because they were unable to survive due to their changing environment, they could not adapt therefore they could not survive. We are no different; we need to change with the times, change is necessary. You may need to change aspects of your personal life and your character. In terms of your education, you may have to change your school or classes; or, if you are in college, even your major. Ultimately you must always be prepared to adapt to change.

If you really want to make a change in your life, and make a change for the better, then stop what you are doing now and analyze your life and where you are headed. Ask yourself if this is where you want to go, is this where you want to be, and make a commitment to make a change for the better.

MOVE ON TO BETTER THINGS

Know when it is time to leave, either a relationship, a job, or a place. Never overstay your welcome, always try to leave under good terms and leave doors open. Never burn your bridges in case you need to return. Like with everything in life, there will come a time to leave and move on to bigger and better things. If you feel a situation is getting nasty, then leave. If you feel that there is no more room to advance in your present job, leave. If you feel you have maxed out and are not being challenged anymore, it is time to make a change and leave. If things are not up to your standards, if a relationship is unhealthy, leave. If you feel something is not working out, leave. Leave before a storm is created. If you sense trouble is brewing, leave. Remember to leave quietly so no one gets their feelings hurt, unless you need to explain to someone why you are leaving. Sometimes things can change for the better when you explain your reasons for leaving, but sometimes you just have to move on to bigger and better things.

DETERMINE WHAT IS CREDIBLE

*A*ppearances are very important, not only in the way people think, but also how they look. There are true and false appearances. Never be fooled by false appearances. Things are often not as they seem, so do your own research and gather all evidence before you form your opinion. Find what the real motives are behind the actions, what is behind the mask or the smoke screen. Pay attention to what people are really saying, doing, and to what is going on around you. Understand what the real message is, and never take things at face value. Determine what degree of information is credible, since appearances can be very misleading, and people may be hiding their true intentions. Analyze what you are seeing and hearing, and determine the true nature of a person or a situation. Watch out for those individuals that only promise but don't deliver, who say one thing and do another, and people who only appear to be your friends.

DO NOT ASSUME ANYTHING

Sometimes we get in to trouble for assuming things. Assuming is supposing something without having proof. At times we assume nothing will happen, and other times we assume there will be no consequences, but we should never assume anything. Never assume the other vehicle is going to stop just because the light is red. Never assume that someone will come to your rescue. Never suppose that you have been heard clearly and your message has been understood. Never assume your job is secure, or that you're irreplaceable, or that things will last forever. Never assume that you are always going to win or have it your way. Never assume that you will never be hurt, in life you cannot assume anything. Never assume that you know what others want or that they will always say the truth. Always confirm everything yourself, and do not assume anything because assumptions can and will get you in trouble.

KEEP YOUR IMAGE IMPECCABLE

Personal image speaks volumes about us. Keep your image impeccable. Always preserve a positive image by presenting yourself in a professional and respectable manner. Sell your image by being careful of what you say or do, the way you act, the people you socialize with, the company you keep, who you hang around with, the way you dress, the way you conduct yourself, and the way others perceive you. Protect your image by maintaining your vehicle clean. If you are employed, the same goes for your office, your workstation; things will run smoother if they are clean and organized.

Dress to impress, presentation is important. First impressions do matter and count the most. Whether it is for a job interview, school or school activity like a play, always dress accordingly. Sometimes you may need to blend in or stand out. Always try to know ahead of time what the dress code is. Do not feel afraid to ask if the event or occasion calls for formal, casual, business casual, or professional attire.

THINK BEFORE YOU ACT

Critical thinking means to make an objective analysis and evaluation of a situation or issue in order to form your judgment. Critical thinking is very important. You need to examine, discern, evaluate, and assess before you speak. Think before you act and commit. Simply think before you say yes. Think before you make important decisions or your final choice. Think before you speak, choose and use your words wisely. Stop and think before you offend or before you answer. Always say you will consider it, sleep on it. Never buy something out of impulse, instead take time to think it over and consider all your options. Before committing to anything think and consider all consequences, positive and negative ones. Avoid group thinking because if everyone is thinking the same way, than nobody is really thinking. Never commit to anything or anyone unless you are certain. Give yourself the time necessary to analyze things, the situation and get back to someone about your decision.

A SURVIVAL INSTINCT

*F*ear may be one of our best companions. Fear is what keeps us alive. It is the fear of failure that pushes us to succeed. If you are a student, fear of failing exams may force you to study harder or to complete your homework. The fear of being grounded may cause you to obey your parents. The possibility of suspension may make you follow the rules at school and doing what is required. The fear of injury keeps you from being reckless.

There are many different kinds of things you may fear. Among them may be diseases or illnesses, breaking the law, ruining relationships, financial insecurity, infringing moral rules, and losing respect, credibility or a good reputation.

Most of these fears can lead you to make good decisions, live good lives, and stay out of trouble in general. Following safety and legal rules keeps you alive and out of prison. It is when you lose these fears that you may be in danger of trouble because you become fearless, and this could result in terrible consequences. Prisons and cemeteries are already full of brave individuals who lost their fear, so it's best to be fearful but free and alive. See fear as that friend and companion that keeps you from making poor choices. Fear is a human quality, and nobody can take it away; it is a God-given survival instinct.

CHALLENGES
SITUATIONS THAT TEST YOUR ABILITIES

Welcome the challenges that life brings, they are the tasks or situations that test your abilities. Life is full of challenges. God is always going to challenge us with difficulties. Think of them as quizzes and tests that prepare you for life, for what's ahead, the final exam.

Life is all about challenges. Without challenges life would be very boring. Challenges are what makes life fun and exciting, and brings out the best in all of us. Challenges are the reason you get up each morning to conquer and overcome them. Challenge yourself with something new every day; today's pains are tomorrow's gains, so develop your full potential. Your ability to handle challenges will determine your character, and the kind of person you develop into. Overcoming adversity will make you a better person, wiser, more compassionate, more caring, stronger, more confident, and more experienced. What seemed challenging yesterday, will be a walk in the park tomorrow.

Challenges will keep you growing. When someone repeats the same thing each day, it just means they are no longer being challenged; they are stuck in a rut, or a comfort zone. They are due for a change, a new challenge, but some people are afraid of change or new challenges. To achieve success you need challenges. Doing the same things over and over again will teach you nothing. You learn when you are challenged by new things; therefore, embrace challenges, change and the new. Challenges are accomplishing what others said could not be done in order to succeed, so where others have failed you need to be creative. Never wait to hit bottom to make a change. If you feel you are going down the wrong path, stop and seek help. Or if you are lost ask for help. Recall, the changes you make today will define who you become tomorrow.

God may place difficult people in your path to challenge you. But remember that difficult people will teach you the best lessons, just like difficult situations, they help you grow. Challenges will make you more responsible, wiser, and stronger. They keep you moving forward. You need challenges in your life, think of them as stepping stones that help bring you closer to your goals.

LOOK FOR OPPORTUNITIES

*A*n opportunity is a set of circumstances that makes it possible to do something. Look for opportunities in everything. Take every opportunity that is presented to you, and make the best of it. Be prepared when opportunities arise, and think of them as possibilities. Where others may see only barriers, you need to see opportunities. Create your own opportunities.

Obstacles, on the other hand, are what you will have instead of opportunities if you take your eyes off your goals. Consider obstacles as opportunities to get you back on track. Reflect on how you will proceed to move these obstacles or whatever is blocking your path. Draw a straight line to your goals and do not let anything stop you. Do not allow obstacles to get in the way of your goal. Some opportunities come only once in a lifetime. Obstacles prevent or hinder your progress, while opportunities encourage it and facilitate it.

CHARACTER

GOD MADE US THIS WAY FOR HIS PURPOSE

As a young person, developing your character to become the person you want to be should be among your top priorities. Work on building your character. Your character is the sum of your mental and moral qualities that make you different from others. We all have distinctive and different qualities that set us apart from the rest of the crowd. Each person is different; God made us this way for His purpose. Some people may think you are weird, but you are just different. You have your own character, strengths, weaknesses, sense of humor and so forth. These characteristics represent who you are; embrace them, and make the best of them.

Do not live life according to others. Dare to be different and original, to stand out and think differently. Be unique. Be what you want to be, don't let others dictate who you should be, or place limitations on you. Do not be afraid to stand out or go a different route.

WHAT DO YOU PORTRAY?

Character and personality are similar, but they are not the same. Personality refers to your inborn traits while character is learned behavior. Attitudes can change from time to time, but personality is you. What kind of personality do you have? What do people see in you? What do you portray? How do others perceive you? Personality lies in the way you conduct yourself and the ability you have to make friends. Personality traits can include being charismatic, joyful, compassionate, genuine and sincere, these are qualities that attract people to you. A great personality attracts people. If you have a friendly personality and are very social, you'll interest others with your conversation. When you are easy to get along with, confident, life of the group, and you choose your words wisely, you'll have that something in you that makes people like and follow you. With a great personality people will like you because you are very outgoing and engaging. Work on your personality; your personality will carry you.

DON'T BE A WHINER

You have the choice to make things better for you and your loved ones. Going through life complaining about everything will get you nowhere. Don't live complaining about things that just don't matter, and complaining just to complain or looking for things to whine about; simply make the best of it and move on. Do not feel sorry for yourself, there is no use for being unhappy about what cannot be undone; learn from mistakes and begin doing something new or different. Don't waste valuable time and energy whining, or sitting around feeling sorry for yourself, licking your own wounds. Get up, shake off the dust and move on!

Some people tend to go through life complaining about every little thing. Even if there is nothing to complain about they will find something to whine about. For some people it is always either too cold or too hot; too high or too low; too fast or too slow; too close or too far. This could be contagious, avoid negative people, and get away from them. They will stress you out and drain your energy. Also some people go through life complaining about their present situation, but do nothing to change it. These people are very toxic, get as far away from them as you can.

Moving on is a matter of integrating life's disappointments, sadness and injustices, so instead of becoming obstacles, they can serve as the foundation for growth.

WALK TALL AND SMILE

*C*onfidence can be defined as a feeling of self-assurance that arises from you when you realize your own abilities or qualities to accomplish something. Have confidence in yourself, in what you do and stand for. You may have confidence in some areas and not in others, so draw from those areas where you are self-assured.

At all times know where you are headed. Never push your luck or go too far. Do not overdo it, know your limitations and trust yourself. Confidence needs to be earned. Trust your abilities, be prepared, rehearse, and do not grow cocky. Once you make the decision to make a move; proceed forward with the utmost confidence. Speak and show confidence. Raise your head high, shoulders back and walk confidently towards your goal. Walk tall and smile.

DO NOT MAKE UP EXCUSES

*M*ake every action a success, if you said you would do something then do it, follow through, set your mind to it, and you will accomplish it. Take the word "no" out of your vocabulary. The first time it's an innocent mistake; the second time it is a stupid choice.

Never try to justify your bad actions, your bad behavior, and your failures with excuses. It is always easier to find excuses rather than find solutions or results. Sometimes we make up excuses for our failure. Excuses as to why we did this and not that, why we skip or quit school altogether, and why we failed at life. Fifty percent is mental, and the other fifty percent is physical, so prepare your mind and body, and stop making up excuses. By making excuses you have lost the first part of the battle, the mental part. You need to believe in yourself!

If you look at reasons to fail you will find them, if you look at reasons to succeed you will also find them, if you want something bad enough you will find a way to achieve it, and if not, you will find an excuse. Be honest with yourself and others. Take responsibility and try to understand the real reasons behind your excuses. This will move you closer to achieving your goals.

MATURITY

ASSUME YOUR ROLE

*I*nitiative is one of the clearest signs a young person is reaching maturity. If your parents or teachers have to be reminding you less each time about the things you are responsible for (chores, personal hygiene, completing homework, and so forth), you are showing signs of maturity.

Maturity means you start living a productive life, like a mature tree that starts producing fruit, and it's now ripe and no longer green. For a youngster like you, maturing means you need to stop playing games with your life and start making intelligent decisions. Perhaps now you have a part-time job and are looking into colleges and universities to continue your education. Good behavior comes with rewards, while bad behavior has no rewards, only negative consequences. Life does not reward stupidity. If you are to survive in this world you need to master adult-like behavior, and always look at things from a different perspective. You can choose to go through life being young and stupid or older and wiser. Be watchful of your conduct.

Young man, young woman, you are leaving your childhood and your adolescence behind and becoming a fully responsible adult. You are now older and you need to assume your role. You are developing into a man or woman, not only in your physical body but your mind as well, your way of thinking and the way you perceive things. Maturing is not just physical, but you are also maturing mentally, emotionally and spiritually.

We all go through our childhood like normal kids, but some people seem to never grow up and they continue to behave like children their entire lives. Believing the world needs to cater to them and their needs. But maturity means you start acting your age, you set an example for the younger ones who will follow, and you are able to control your emotions and behavior. Continue showing initiative and taking responsibility for your life, your actions, and your future.

CHOOSE RIGHT OVER WRONG

Doing the right thing is doing what is ethical or just. Oftentimes, you may worry more about what others may think or say, than about doing the right thing. Maybe it is because you are trying to impress someone, or you are with the minority and are afraid of being criticized or expelled from your group or circle of friends. Always do what you feel is right, what you feel in your heart to be correct, and do not be pressured into making bad decisions. Always think of the consequences of your actions: Are you hurting yourself or others with your actions? Do not do things just because you believe everyone else is doing them. Do what you were taught by your parents or teachers. Simply do the right thing, even when nobody is watching, and do not be afraid of critics. Remember two wrongs do not make a right. Influence others to do well, choose right over wrong. Always strive to make a difference.

Have people expressed disapproval of you or something you did based on your perceived faults or mistakes? That's called criticism. Think for a moment how criticism has made you feel and how you have reacted to being criticized. Chances are criticism has made you feel inadequate, hurt, stupid, or angry. Perhaps you have even been discouraged from continuing to do something you like after being criticized by someone.

Because of the impact you know criticism causes in people, the last thing you want to do is go around criticizing others. It is a fact that there are some people who spend their entire life criticizing other people or their actions regardless of what they do, good or bad, or indifferent. There are people who do not do anything productive with their lives except criticize others. Learn by heart that it is not your job to criticize! Before you criticize think about what the other person might be going through, perhaps loss of job, a home or a loved one, a divorce, or failed an important exam. Before you criticize drug addicts, homeless people, women on the streets, and others, remember these are someone's loved ones.

An antidote to destructive criticism is seeing others as your equal. Do not treat others as inferior or as of less importance than you. Do not see them as if what they do or stand for is of less value or importance, or that their group is inferior and of less importance. Whether it is race, religion, social status or occupation, do your best not to make others feel inferior. Don't make them feel as if your job is more important than theirs, do not treat people different just because they do not look or dress the same as you, or have different beliefs or values..

Constructive criticism, on the other hand, consists in offering valid and well-reasoned opinions about your work and the work of others. It involves both positive and negative comments, but it's made in a friendly way rather than a judgmental one. Give and receive constructive criticism. This will help you improve your life and the lives of others.

Do not let negative criticism bring you down or make you stop you from pursuing your goals. If you get criticized about being crazy, it's okay because crazy people with crazy ideas are the ones that make the world go round. Your crazy idea today may not seem as crazy tomorrow. You may be an innovator. When people talk about you or criticize you, be happy you are on people's minds, you are important, you are staying current. Criticism may be a sign they are really interested in you and what you do, that they admire you, they are afraid of you, of your competition, and they are watching your moves. It's when they forget about you that you need to worry.

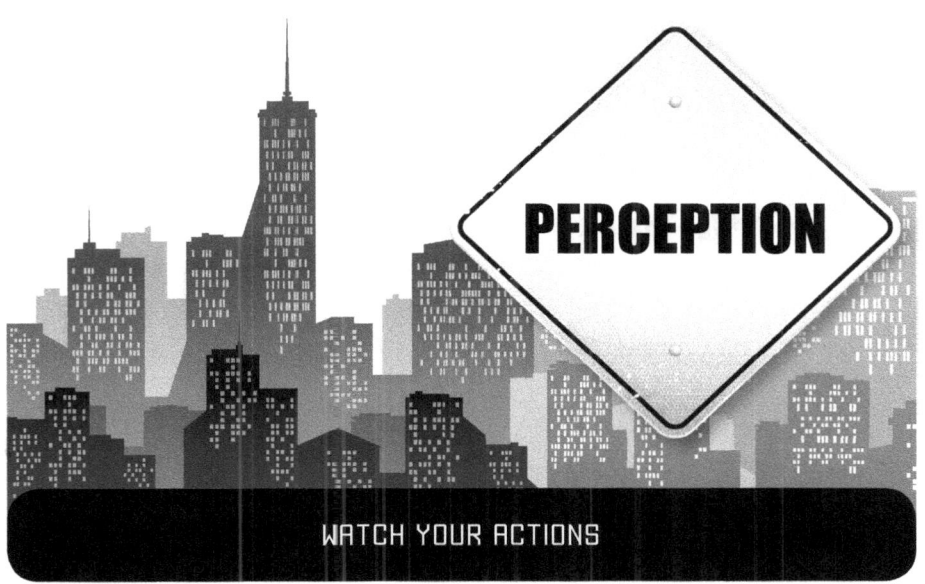

WATCH YOUR ACTIONS

*P*erception is a way of regarding, understanding, or interpreting something. Perception is reality, it's the way people perceive you and it is what they see that counts. Always watch your actions, the way you conduct yourself, your image. Remember beauty is in the eyes of the beholder, what may seem beautiful to you may not seem so attractive to others. You may have a group of people looking at the exact same thing and each will see it differently. The same group of people may be listening to the same exact speech and each one will hear a whole different message, remember we all see and hear only what we want to see and hear based on our perception.

SOMEONE WE CAN COUNT ON

A person who is reliable is a person who is trustworthy. Always be reliable, someone who can always be counted on. You could be the greatest worker or athlete on earth, but if you are unreliable it doesn't matter how great you are; nobody will want you on their team. We need people who are reliable, someone we can count on to be there no matter what, rain or shine, someone who is consistent, and trustworthy. People need to be able to count on you all the time, day in and day out.

DO NOT BE ENVIOUS

The dictionary tells us that contentment is a mental or emotional state of satisfaction drawn from being at ease in one's situation. If you have accepted your situation, you have contentment in your life. Contentment is a form of humble happiness.

Relative deprivation is you comparing yourself to others. We cannot go through life wanting what others have. This is dangerous; it is bad for your health, whether you are envious of others' success, relationships, material things, good looks or good luck. It is a fact of life we cannot all have everything; you cannot go through life being jealous of others' achievements; envy is a very destructive emotion, it's like a disease. Face it, we will always encounter people who are better than us; accept it. Envy, greed and jealousy are all diseases, they are signs of insecurity, weakness, and obsessions. Avoid jealousy and count your own blessings, rather than counting others' blessings. Oftentimes, envy makes us feel inferior, but instead of being envious, let it motivate you to surpass them or equal them, or better yourself. Always do your best not to stir up envy, try not to show off or flaunt your good fortune, whether it is jewelry, cars, looks or talents. Do not act perfect or without faults, show you are one of the same and help others.

Sometimes for your own good it is wise to disguise or camouflage your good fortune or wealth, show some defects to show you are also not perfect. Show sympathy to others and do not brag or show off, simply say, "Maybe I just got lucky." Sometimes it is best to hide your skills and qualities, and maybe show some weakness. Comparing yourself to others will only get you stressed and depressed. Remember life will give you everything but not all at once. Being content with what you have does not mean you shouldn't aim to be a better person and have better things. It simply means you do not have a constant ambition for more, or a desire to have what others have achieved in their life.

AVOID BAD HABITS

When you have a usual way of behaving, something that you often do regularly and repeatedly is called a habit. As you have developed into a young person, you may have noticed that you have good and bad habits. Most of us do.

Bad habits are hard to break. It is always best to not start with bad habits early in life. Oftentimes, we pick up a bad habit without even noticing it. Other habits are more noticeable such as smoking, drugs or alcohol. Sometimes it's voluntarily but other times it's involuntarily. There are patterns and indicators to warn us of a habit forming, often it is learned and done unconsciously without thought. It's always best to avoid habits that are bad and destructive. Promote good habits; these always start at home. To break a bad habit try and replace it with a good habit. If you drink soda regularly for example, try replacing it with water or tea. If you eat a lot of junk food at school or work, replace it with a healthy sack lunch from home or eat a good, healthy breakfast or lunch before you leave home. This will also help you save money for other things you might need. If you are addicted to being online all the time, try replacing whatever you are watching with something educational, motivational, inspirational, or something related to what you want to study or learn. Good habits will form over time as you continually repeat them.

COMPOSURE

KEEP YOUR COOL

When you are calm and in control of yourself you have composure. Composure is vital. Always stay composed no matter what circumstances you encounter. Do not lose your cool. Cooler heads always prevail. At all times maintain your composure; it's what's inside of you that matters, the way you feel inside. Do not allow your present environment or situation to change you or control who you are, take charge and change your environment. Do not permit the world to change you, be a world changer! Make it better! Look for the good in everything, and be thankful for all the good in your life. Be grateful and thank God for what you do have.

INSPIRE OTHERS

When you feel stimulated to do something, especially something creative, you are being inspired. When you have been inspired by others to achieve something, and achieve it, you can become an inspiration yourself. Be an inspiration to others. Inspire them to succeed, to overcome, to continue in their struggle, to better themselves, and to learn. Be an example for others to follow in your footsteps, to do well and do the right thing. Inspire them to not give up hope, to speak up, to write, to get involved, to help, to give and not be afraid. Find your own inspiration, and be an inspiration for others.

MAKE YOUR PARENTS PROUD

The parent's job is to prepare you for life. Sometimes parents need to be firm, to get their message across and get you to understand. They tell you what you need to hear, not what you want to hear, and teach what you need to know and not what you want to know, what you need to learn and not what you want to learn, to give you what you need and not what you want.

After you are born, parents make many changes in their lives to accommodate yours. They do this to ensure you are safe and have a good life. Everything parents do is with their child in mind. They work hard for you. They would give their life for you, so respect your parents and value them since they only want what is best for you.

When you hurt yourself by your actions, you also hurt them. Parents only want what is best for you. They work hard for you so you may have a better life. You need to appreciate all their efforts since they only want what is best for you, and everything they do is with you in mind. Parents worry about their kids' wellbeing, be thankful that they are concerned about your future. Appreciative and value them. Sometimes we do not want to hear the truth, but we need to hear the truth from our parents even if it hurts. Keep in mind your parents will not be around forever, eventually you will be on your own.

Often we hear teens say, "I hate my parents, I can't wait until I am eighteen so I can leave the house and nobody can tell me what to do anymore!" We think life is easy and that we do not need our parents anymore, and that we can survive on our own working at the fast-food joint. Guess what? Unless you get an education and are able to make a decent salary, life will be very miserable for you. Oftentimes, teens will leave their home only to find the reality of life and end up having to come back home. Sometimes you may do things to hurt your parents but you are only hurting yourself. We need to stop being *ungrateful*, and see all they do for us. We tend to sometimes take advantage of the fact that our parents love us, and will do anything for us. Being a parent is one of the toughest jobs in the world, but too often we do not see it or start to appreciate parents until it is too late or until we become parents ourselves.

Parents do their best to prepare you for life, so listen to them. Keep in mind the best lessons are taught at home by your parents. Education originates at home, and continues at home. You need to trust your parents with your problems, questions or concerns but often we rather listen to our friends because "they know more." This can lead you into trouble so you need to ask yourself, "Am I prepared to face the world alone once my parents are gone?" Because once you are on your own, it is a whole different ball game when they are no longer around to save you, to fix what breaks, to give you money, to bail you out every time you are in trouble, to comfort you when you are sick or need their advice.

Do you have the tools that you need to survive? When you are young you feel that your needs come first before everything else. But once you are on your own you will quickly find out that you will no longer get it your way, that the world owes you nothing, and that you now have to earn everything you want because your parents are no longer there to provide it to you. We want the freedom, but once that freedom comes, we do not know what to do with it. We feel lost and confused, not knowing who to turn to for help.

Always do your best to make your parents proud, even if they are no longer with you. Before you do something ask yourself, "Would this make my parents proud or would they be ashamed of my actions?" And always remember if at least once in your life you did not feel like you hated your parents, than they probably did not do a very good job of raising you.

FAULTS

DO NOT BLAME OTHERS

*I*t seems like every time something goes wrong in our life our first reaction is to find someone to blame other than ourselves. We tend to refuse to take responsibility for our actions, "Surely someone else must have caused this or that which caused me to fail."

You may try to convince yourself it was not your fault, "it is never my fault" is your first reaction, but unless you are willing to take full responsibility for your own actions, you will never grow as an individual. You will never learn, just like an alcoholic or drug addict when they try to hide the fact that they have a problem. The first step to recovery is for the person to recognize and admit that he/she has a problem if the person really wants to be rehabilitated and make a full recovery. Same goes for when you are wrong, you need to recognize it, accept it, learn from it, make it right if possible and move on. If you know you have done something wrong or made a mistake, do not look for someone to blame, simply admit your error, apologize and move on, and do not commit the same error again. Apologizing is a sign of courage and of strength. There is no reward for finding faults, only for finding solutions, so finger pointing and accusing others will get you nowhere. You cannot go through life blaming others for your faults, mishaps, mistakes, failures, or your wrong choices. It is not your parent's fault or your teacher's fault, it's not your friend's fault either; it's the result of bad choices that you made that landed you where you are.

Keep in mind that you will not always get everything your way, or will be first all the time, or obtain what you want. Never believe things will just fall on your laps or that things will last forever. Under no circumstances place the blame on others for your problems, learn that in life you will need to work for everything. We are the ones who determine the outcome of our lives; we are the only ones who have control over it. To make a change do not go through life feeling self-pity, take control of your life now and steer in the direction you want to go, not where life takes you. Do not be like a ship in the ocean without sails, being tossed wherever the wind and waves take you with no direction, no destination, no purpose, and no guidance. Do not wait for tomorrow and take action now. If you procrastinate you will lose valuable time, the longer you wait the farther you will drift and run the possibility of sinking. Sink or swim, your time is now, your future is now, so begin preparing for it. Figure out what you want to be and why.

Do not blame others for your problems. Take charge and ownership of your life, your education, career, health, and your destination. Take responsibility for your conduct and choose your path wisely.

RISKY TRENDS

STAY SAFE AND HEALTHY

There are many cool and popular trends that young people follow. Some of these trends are fine, and maybe part of cultural or fashion movements that every generation has. Others are bad and risky trends that you should stay away from in order to stay safe and healthy. Let's see some of these dangerous tendencies among teenagers and young adults.

Some of the consequences of Internet or social media addiction, are sleep deprivation and obesity. Posting everything about your life on social networks can also lead to cyberbullying. Bullying is defined as aggressive behavior by an individual that causes discomfort to another individual. Trolling is another way of bullying, and this is defined as the act of deliberately inflicting hatred, bigotry, or racism. Cyberbullying can cause depression, anxiety, severe isolation, and even suicide.

Thirty-nine percent of teens on social networks have been

cyberbullied, compared to twenty-two percent of teens who do not use social networks (Pew Research Center). Another term that may be new to us is "Facebook depression," which is defined as emotional disturbance that develops when teens and pre-teens spend a great deal of time on social media sites. Spending so much time on media sites causes you to lose your privacy and disconnect from reality. By posting your personal life on social media you leave digital fingerprints which can have serious repercussions in your future, both your professional and personal life.

Statistics show teens who check Facebook every fifteen minutes while doing their homework are getting lower grades. Social networks have a bad effect on teen's intelligence and results in a shorter attention span.

Sometimes teens get distracted to this type of sites to kill boredom in their study times. Social networks have become and unhealthy addiction for teens, which can result in loss of privacy and safety, where you can become a victim to harassment and abuse. Sexting — the act of sending someone sexually explicit photographs or messages via your cell phone— can also have awful consequences. You can even be charged with child pornography. Remember that what goes online, stays online, and as result any future job or even your college acceptance is placed in jeopardy. Remember that Facebook is a permanent record. Other statistics show teens who use social media on a regular basis are more likely to use tobacco, alcohol or drugs. Also, avid users of social media tend to be unhappy.

Gaming can become another addiction, which results in lack of social interaction. Obsessive gaming can have long-term social consequences.

Teens addicted to gaming will not develop effective social skills, which will hinder their ability to develop and maintain healthy relationships in college and beyond. Suddenly you will be a twenty-one-year-old with the social skills of a fifteen-year-old. One of the scariest consequences of addicted gamers is that often they try to imitate the characters in these games, and act out violently towards others. Violent games can lead to higher risk of violent behavior among teens. Violent games are the most popular among teens. Brief exposure to violent games increases aggressive thoughts, feelings and behavior.

The latest Pew Research Center survey shows three out of four people between the ages of eighteen and forty have a tattoo. Out of that number, fifty-nine percent are female. Remember to protect your image, think twice about getting that tattoo or body piercing. Any type of marking on your body will have terrible consequences in both your professional and personal life. Think about how you will be perceived by others. Putting the name of your girlfriend or boyfriend on your body may not be such a good idea. Consider how long you will be attached to this person, and how will your next boyfriend or girlfriend feel about you having someone else's name tattooed on your skin. Piercings along with tattoos can also lead to diseases. And all this costs money, so instead save the money for school. Most people who get tattoos or piercings end up regretting it. Remember, you are special and beautiful just the way God created you; therefore, you do not need other ornaments.

Last but not least, let's talk about reckless driving. First of all, driving a vehicle is a privilege, not a right, so take care of it. When you get your driver's license you will have more responsibility. Just because you can drive does not mean you can be out at night hanging out with your friends or giving them rides. Do not abuse this privilege.

You have an obligation to your parents to take care of the car you are driving, and do not try to show off in front of your friends by speeding or driving recklessly. Never forget that the privilege to drive also costs money. This means the car insurance policy will go up. Be safe and avoid getting any tickets which could result in an increase in policy to your parents.

LEAVE YOUR MARK

Your happiness should not be tied to people or things you can lose, like money or material things. Money cannot buy you happiness, because happiness is free. If you measure success by how much money you make, or how many toys you have, you will live a very miserable life. You will never be happy.

Success is about doing what makes you happy, feeling good inside and being content with your accomplishments. Success is not necessarily about material things, it could be your education. Sadly though, too often many try to take the easy way out when it comes to their education, they make up excuses for not staying in school, for not pursuing an education, and for not succeeding. You may try to convince yourself that you are not capable and just act incompetent only to be left alone by others. The fact of the matter is that when we are born our brain is similar to a blank computer hard drive ready to be filled with whatever information we want to write on it. We learn by watching, reading, listening, feeling, but sometimes we avoid learning because we are preoccupied with other things that don't matter. We learn what interests us, we may pick up curse words easier than other words, we develop bad habits faster than good ones, and we may feel that we do not need an education because we believe that we can survive without it. Learning is a choice. You can choose to be intelligent by educating yourself or remain ignorant. You can focus on your studies and learn or not pay attention and refuse to learn. We come up with excuses to justify our lack of learning. But one of the ways we learn is by reading repetition, also through trial and error, and if you want to learn something, set your mind to it. You will find ways to learn even if it means reading the same book a few times until it sinks in, or taking notes of the words you may not understand, or phrases that at first don't make sense. Do research on whatever subject you are working on, with so much technology and information at our fingertips there is just no excuse for not learning.

Through dedication, persistence and repetition you will get it right, block out all other distractions and focus all of your energy on your task at hand. Education is a choice, and only you can choose education over ignorance. If you are determined to learn, you will learn but you need to have passion for learning, and be able to get into your work. Choose a subject of interest to you and gather all the information, question everything, research it, and add it all up and put it to the test, this is how you gain knowledge.

As we learn we will make mistakes, this is part of the learning process, this is how we learn, and it's called experience. Making mistakes just means you are working, gaining experience and you are learning, the only people that never make mistakes are those who never do anything with their life except criticize what others do. Understand that no one can force you to learn, you can lead a man to knowledge but you can't force him to drink from the cup of knowledge, he has to thirst for knowledge. Be hungry for knowledge because it is powerful, knowledge is the only weapon you need in life, never stop learning and question everything. Make it a habit to learn something new every day. Share what you have learned with others since you will also learn in the process of teaching.

You can spend your entire life reading books and learning, but unless you are willing to practice what you have learned then all of your studying has been in vain, you are wasting your time. It's like planning without action. So practice what you have learned and make it a habit to learn new things each day and then put it into practice. Oftentimes, we know what to do but we just don't do it. For whatever reason it may be we are hesitant or afraid. We fear criticism, isolation, loneliness, disagreement, and conflict. We are afraid of causing waves, of change, or what others will think or say. But if you are serious about your success, then pursue and obtain your education, and go out and change the world, make an impact, leave your mark.

AVOID ENDING UP IN PRISON

*P*rison is a very real and lonely place. Once you end up in prison you lose your freedom, your rights, your family, your job, your privacy, your dignity, and you become nonexistent to the outside world. You become a number, an inmate number, a statistic, and a burden to society. You successfully become someone undesirable to society, no one will pity you, care what you think or what you have to say; your word won't matter anymore, it will be too late to be sorry. Your homeboys, your gang, your crew, your "family" will be no more. Everyone will forget about you, no one will visit you, write to you, check on your wellbeing, or send money, except maybe your real family. That's only if you are lucky enough to have a family that hasn't abandoned or turned their back on you. Depending on your crime and how it affected your family, you may no longer have one. Sadly, even they will turn against you and abandon you. The saddest part of it all is that nobody will really care how bad or tough or brave you were.

Most of the tough inmates in prison today did not land there by accident; there were steps or missteps that landed them in prison. The majority of these men or women started on the wrong path since they were children. It all began with not listening to their parents, not having respect for anything or anyone. Indeed, these were once children who did not care about rules, house or school rules, they did not care about their family or the suffering they would cause through their actions. These individuals who were once kids did not care about laws, they felt and decided that these rules did not apply to them; they decided they would make their own rules or laws as they went along in life. Nothing else mattered and they did as they pleased. They convinced themselves they would never be caught because they were too smart, "I am not stupid like the rest, and I ain't no fool! They only catch the dumb ones; I got street-smart; I will do things my way; I will take the easy route to success; I will take a shortcut to success; I will break the rules; I will make my own rules; and, nothing will happen to me."

Most likely, when parents tried to get these kids to do something, their response was, "No, I don't want to" or, "you can't make me." As they grew older their disobedience progressed from not listening to their parents to not listening to teachers, and finally not listening to the law. It may have started with simple things like not wanting to eat their dinner, wear the clothes bought for them, getting off the phone when told, or they began coming home after curfew. They rebelled and disobeyed, talked back to their parents and gave their friends more importance. When parents would threaten to discipline them they would say, "If you touch me I will call the police and tell them you hit me and they will arrest you." If parents tried to talk to them, they would say, "I do not want to hear it, I am tired of listening to your mouth, and I do not feel like talking to you!" Or when asked to listen when their parents would try to explain something to them, they would say, "I do not want to hear it! I know everything." When told to be quiet or turn down their music, their response was, "No, I do not want to and you cannot make me." When parents would walk into their room they would say, "You need to knock, I want privacy... Get out of my room." When asked to clean their room they would say "No, I will clean it when I want to clean it." These are only examples of a rebellious start that will lead to a lifetime of rebellion. Obeying and honoring your parents is a command from God because it carries blessings. Whereas disobedience carries negative results that may lead to rebellion against the law, which will lead to prison.

Once you land in prison, guess what? All the rules change because you no longer have choices. Remember, on the outside you had choices but in prison you no longer have choices. Choices are obsolete. You will eat what you are told and when you are told. I hope you like vegetables and animal parts blended together, with no taste, because in prison they do not care about how food tastes, food preferences or food allergies; they only need to meet calorie set guidelines. They do not care about pleasing your taste palate; you will eat what you are served and you will like it. You will also shower when you are told, and in front of everyone; too bad if you are shy because privacy no longer exists. You will wear what you are told to wear and I hope you like orange or stripes because this will be your new wardrobe. You will use the phone when they allow you to use it and it comes with a time limit, and that is if you have money in your account to pay for it. In prison, just like on the outside, things cost, and if you don't have the money you are screwed. They will listen in on all your conversations, read all your letters and messages, tell you what pictures you can and cannot have. They will tell you what music you can and cannot listen to and how loud. When they speak you will listen, you will speak when you are allowed to speak and only as long as they allow you. They will tell you what books you can and cannot read; what programs on television you can and cannot watch, and that's only if you are lucky enough to have a television because in prison these are very expensive luxuries that most prisoners cannot afford, or are even allowed to have. These are considered privileges and they have to be earned. In prison you can lose all privileges that took months or years to earn. You can lose them in a second.

They watch your every move even while you go to the bathroom. In prison you will go to bed when they tell you to go to bed, they will raid your room, your cell, go through all your belongings and take what they want, and there is nothing you can do. Other prisoners will take your stuff as well and there is nothing you can do about it. In prison everything is lost including your innocence. You might be abused and raped on a regular basis, maybe for as long as you are in prison, your dignity and pride will be gone. They will decide who visits you and for how long, and they can suspend your visits as they please. If you get sick you may have to wait for days, weeks or months to receive basic medical attention. You will have to wait a long time, wait your turn to be attended, and some inmates die waiting for that medical treatment that never came, because they do not care about you or your health. Prison guards have no pity, they get paid to be there, they get to go home after their shift, and you will not be able to leave.

Think about it for a minute: Everything you refused to do on the outside, you will be forced to do in prison but to the extreme because the prison will own you. Everything you took for granted on the outside will be a faraway dream, and if this is not bad enough if you misbehave in prison, in the hole you will go. Twenty-three hours a day by yourself with no human contact. You will sleep, eat, shower, and use the bathroom in this small, ten by ten, cell that has no windows, no sunlight, and you will not know if it is day or night. You may get one hour of recreation in the dog kennel if you behave; it is like another prison inside a prison, and all because you did not allow yourself to be disciplined at home.

In prison life stands still while life on the outside goes on. People will go on with their lives, they will forget about you, and you will become nonexistent to them. If you have a girlfriend/boyfriend, guess what, she/he will become someone else's girlfriend/ boyfriend. Your partner may promise to wait for you, but in reality no one waits for someone, life goes on except for yours. Also someone is now wearing your clothes, driving your car, living in your house. For prisoners life stands still, and there is nothing you can do if you land in prison. You will be caged up in four walls like a wild animal, not able to leave, and without any rights. You gave up those rights when you decided to disobey the law and make your own rules because you thought you were bad and did not care about discipline; well, now the penitentiary system will discipline you, and they will have no mercy on you. There is nothing you can do, you have no choice, no voice, no vote, no rights, freedom is now just a dream, you lost your privacy, your pride, your dignity, and now you just sit in your cell feeling sorry for yourself hoping it is just a nightmare from where you want to wake up but you cannot. Don't let this become your reality.

If this does become your reality the system will now discipline you, because they now own you, and they will show you no mercy or compassion because the system makes money off of you. Each bed that is occupied is more money for them, so they do not care if you ever leave. It is all job security for them to make you mess up and prolong your stay. And you may ask yourself, "How did I get here?" Well let's backtrack. Let us review where you went wrong along the way. There were hints, clues, sometimes we can often trace our problems back to one bad decision. Maybe a person started you on this path; you listened to this person instead of our parents, because you failed to see that they were a bad influence and didn't stay away from them. When they told you to take those drugs, drink that alcohol, break those windows, steal that car, assault that person, paint that wall, break the law, told you nothing would happen and to not be a wimp... You chose to listen to your so-called friends, instead of your parents or your teachers. And now, these so-called friends have impacted your life in a negative way for the rest of your life. Sadly, you will never see them again unless they end up in the same prison. So rather than listening to your parents you listened to other people who did not love you or have your best interest in mind.

One thing that you should always remember is that nobody can force you to do anything you do not want to do. You do not need to belong to a gang to survive; you do not need those homeboys, your second "family," or your crew; belonging to these groups will only bring you more problems. Once you join a gang you are a marked man for life, even if you decide you no longer want to belong to a gang, you will need to watch your back. You will have problems that you never had before until you became involved with them and they became your ticket to prison.

If and when you do get out of prison your troubles are not over yet, oh no, you will still be on probation for years or maybe life. You may still owe restitution and, depending on your crime, it could be into the thousands maybe even millions of dollars. So in other words, you may be in debt to society and to your victims for the rest of your life. And the system will not be done with you because obligations to society will need to be fulfilled like probation, restitution, and depending on the crime you may need to register as an offender. You will never be allowed to own firearms, you will not be allowed to vote, and you may not be able to live where you want to live.

On top of all that, as much as you try to start over, nobody will want to hire you because you have a criminal record. You are now a felon, and nobody is going to trust you. As soon as a prospective employer sees felony conviction on your job resume or job application they will most likely place it in the waste basket. Forget about those good-paying government jobs too. If you are lucky maybe a friend will hire you, that is if you still have friends left, because most will have moved on and forgotten about you or may not want nothing to do with you or be associated with you. If you are lucky enough, a family member may hire you, again if you still have any family left that is willing to support you, willing to help you get back on your feet. Where will you live? Who will take you in? As you can see, you need to look farther ahead before making those bad decisions, look beyond your target, and see what is ahead. Look at the whole picture, and picture the consequences. And see everything not just what you want to see; the choices you make today will have an impact on your life tomorrow and for the rest of your life.

Additionally, consider the pain, suffering and damage you will have caused your loved ones with your careless actions like financial damages, physical, emotional, mental, health, and family damage which will lead to stress, anxiety, and depression. And take into account that most of these damages are irreversible because when you are sentenced to years in prison, it is like your family has also been sentenced to years of prison, years of misery. Their world will also be turned upside down, and it will take a toll on the family, on the marriage, and on your siblings. Sadly, many parents often hear this, "I am only harming myself. Stay out of my life!" But think again. Your actions will take everyone down with you. The damage will be irreversible. You will have lost a beautiful part of your life, the best years of your life will be gone, and you will not be able to recover them. Remember, time is something that you cannot bring back. Sometimes when we end up in trouble we tell ourselves, "If only I would have known, if I could turn back time, if I could undo things, if I could have seen this coming..." Well, the time is now to make the right decisions, it is your time. Your actions now will determine your future. If you are going down the wrong path, STOP NOW! It is never too late to make a change before you sink deeper.

Crime is not a job, it is a disease, and it is very contagious. Get treatment, get cured, because crime does not pay, it only pays those who run the prisons: the lawyers, judges and everyone else in between involved in running the system. Prisons are full of men and women who are by-products of weak, undisciplined, and uneducated children who were not taught right from wrong, or kids that simply refused to learn right from wrong. Remember, you are a by-product of your own actions and therefore, you are not a victim of society.

Always try to do good, do the right thing, walk a straight line, and realize that life has enough complications and challenges as it is, you do not need anymore. Listen to your parents, your teachers, your counselors, your coaches, your elders, your pastors, and your mentors. Do not throw your life away just to impress your friends, or foolishly think people will like you better if you are mischievous. It's your choice, nobody else's. No one ever says, "I want to go to prison when I grow up." Remember that all these individuals in prisons were once kids, yes, kids who would not listen to their parents. If you need help or advice please seek it. You have plenty of resources and people you can turn to like your parents, teachers, coaches, counselors, pastors or wise elders. You are never alone, God is always by your side.

If you need help, ask and seek help, have someone evaluate you. Some kids do not ask for help because they are afraid or too proud, and then they wait until it's too late. This could be due to fear, pride or ignorance, but once kids realize how deep in trouble they are, then they start crying: "Please, your honor give me another chance, I promise I will change." Or, "Please mom and dad help me tell them it was not me, I promise I will change. Just give me another opportunity." But it may be too late; they may have reached the point of no return, where prison is their new reality. And every hardened criminal is a kid crying waiting to be let out, to be set free again, and begging for another chance.

Frequently, we see only what we want to see; we are blinded, and we are fooled into believing what other fools tell us. False promises, false riches, and false idols; you need to value only those things that have value, you need to stop and evaluate yourself and your life. Review your actions now before it is too late, and grade yourself. Are you failing? Self-diagnose your behavior, be objective, be truthful, do not kid yourself, stop before it's too late, before you reach that point of no return. Open your eyes now and see the whole scope of things. The future is in your hands, what will you choose? Success or failure? You decide.

About the Author

Audel Acevedo was born in 1965 in a palm tree hut in a little town in the state of Colima, in Western Mexico. The hut had a dirt floor, and lacked basic services such as running water and electricity. He was one of thirteen children, and was born in extreme poverty. His health was so precarious his family thought he would not survive his first year.

His family immigrated to the United States when he was eight years old. He attended school from fifth to eighth grade in the city of Mesa, Arizona. He was always placed in special education classes because his teachers thought he was "dumb" or "mentally retarded." For his classmates, he was the "dumb kid" who could never get any answers right, and they would laugh at him and his "silly" answers. Eventually he dropped out of school to work as a busboy to help his mother who had separated from his father.

As he publishes this his first book, Acevedo reflects on his life and accomplishments:

> "I have never allowed my past to determine my future, or someone else's opinion of me to define who I am. Even though the odds were stacked against me, I have achieved every goal I set out to achieve, and made each and every one of my dreams come true. And now it's time for me to share what I have learned, and how I managed to overcome and succeed in the face of adversity. I always was what I wanted to be. Everything I set my mind to, I accomplished through persistence and hard work. Some may think I am

intelligent, but I am not; I am persistent.

"At ten years old I had my own paper route, so I had to get up early in the morning to deliver the newspapers before school. When I was thirteen years old I wanted to become a boxer, so I became a boxer. At eighteen I wanted to become a musician, and I became musician. As an adult I wanted to own a restaurant, so I owned a restaurant. I wanted to own my own contracting company, and I still own a contracting company. Since I was a kid I always wanted to travel and see the world, and each year I travel to different destinations; my favorite destination is Havana, Cuba. I always dreamed of living in a big mansion, and I now live in a big, beautiful mansion. I wanted to write my own book, and here it is. And I am already working on a second book.

"I share these success stories not to impress you, but to impress upon you that you too can do it, to inspire you to dream and to live. You too can accomplish whatever you set your mind to. You too can overcome whatever circumstances you may face in life. Whatever you can conceive and believe, you can achieve."

www.ingramcontent.com/pod-product-compliance
Lightning Source LLC
Chambersburg PA
CBHW070656100426
42735CB00039B/2164